QUICK REFERENCE

W9-BYG-126

GUIDE TO

HARD DISK MANAGEMENT

VAN WOLVERTON

PUBLISHED BY
Microsoft Press
A Division of Microsoft Corporation
16011 NE 36th Way, Box 97017, Redmond, Washington 98073-9717

Library of Congress Cataloging in Publication Data

Wolverton, Van, 1939-
Quick reference guide to hard-disk management.
Includes index.
1. File organization (Computer science)   2. Magnetic disks.
I. Title.
QA76.9.F5W65   1988   004.5'6   88-5164
ISBN 1-55615-105-5

Printed and bound in the United States of America.

1 2 3 4 5 6 7 8 9   WAKWAK   3 2 1 0 9 8

Distributed to the book trade in the United States
by Harper & Row.

Distributed to the book trade in Canada by General
Publishing Company, Ltd.

Distributed to the book trade outside the United States
and Canada by Penguin Books Ltd.

Penguin Books Ltd., Harmondsworth, Middlesex, England
Penguin Books Australia Ltd., Ringwood, Victoria, Australia
Penguin Books N.Z. Ltd., 182-190 Wairau Road, Auckland 10,
New Zealand

British Cataloging in Publication Data available

Contents

Introduction v

PART 1: How a Hard Disk Works 1
Types of Hard Disk 1
Inside a Hard Disk 2
Sides, Tracks, and Sectors 3
Installing a Hard Disk 4

PART 2: Preparing Your Hard Disk 7
Finding Out If Your Hard Disk Is Ready to Use 7
Identifying the Hard Disk to DOS — Fdisk 8
Using Fdisk 9
Formatting the Hard Disk 12
Copying the DOS Files to the Hard Disk 13
Testing the Hard Disk 14
A One-Time Process 14

PART 3: Configuring DOS for Your Hard Disk 15
Using the Buffers Configuration Command 16
Need to Use More Files? The Files Configuration Command 17
Need More Drive Letters? The Lastdrive Configuration
    Command 18
Using a RAM Disk 19
Making Your Hard Disk Larger 23
Tailoring Your Startup Procedure with AUTOEXEC.BAT 25

PART 4: Working with Directories 27
Setting Up Your Directories 28
Creating and Removing Directories 29
Keeping Track of Where You Are 31
Moving the DOS Files to a Directory Named \DOS 37
Changing the Way DOS Treats Drives and Directories 41

PART 5: Working with Files 45
Naming Your Files 45
Preventing Accidental Changes and Deletions 47
Copying Files 48
Listing All the Files on the Disk—Tree 55
Some Useful Batch Files.................................... 57

PART 6: Backing Up Your Hard Disk. 65
Back Up Your Program Diskettes............................ 65
Developing a Backup Procedure 66
Using DOS to Back Up Files 66
Controlling the Archive Attribute of a File 75

PART 7: Maintaining Your Hard Disk 77
Leave the System On 77
Keep It Clean 78
What About Surges, Sags, and Spikes? 78
Making Life Easier for Your Hard Disk....................... 79
When You Move Your Computer 81
Installing a New Version of DOS on Your Hard Disk 82

Index 84

Introduction

A hard disk can hold far more data than a diskette can, and DOS, its manager, can move files to and from it much more quickly than it can to and from a diskette. As its name implies, a hard disk isn't flexible like a diskette; typically, data is recorded on one or more rigid metal platters enclosed in a sealed case. A hard disk is also frequently called a fixed disk. Again, as this name implies, you don't remove a fixed disk—it is permanently fixed in the drive.

Because a hard disk can hold so many more files than a diskette, using it effectively requires more planning and housekeeping than using diskettes.

Although a hard disk eliminates the inconvenience of swapping diskettes, and you spend much less time waiting for DOS to find a file or copy it to memory, you have to invest some time in planning how you'll organize your files and in keeping the disk orderly.

It's not unlike keeping track of paper files. When all you have are a couple of dozen file folders with a few sheets of paper in each, you can keep all the files on your desktop. This approach can get aggravating, however, when you have a lot of bulky files and have to shuffle in and around them, searching for what you want.

Switching to a file cabinet gives you more room for files and cleans up your desktop, but if you don't set up some sort of filing system with dividers, hanging file folders, and labeled manila folders, finding the files you need becomes even harder. And when the drawers start filling up—as they always do—you have to go through and thin out the files, tossing the ones you no longer need and putting those you might need later in a storage box.

So it is with computer files, especially when you use a hard disk and several application programs. Files proliferate, and it's all too easy to lose track of the ones you need. But properly organized and managed, a hard disk lets you work significantly faster, with a minimum of fuss. Many tools are available for managing this capacious filing cabinet. Some are as close at hand as your DOS prompt; others come from independent hardware and software providers. Because this reference is not intended as a buyer's guide, and because disk-management needs vary with the ways in which hard disks are used, this book concentrates on DOS commands designed for hard-disk management.

Throughout, the emphasis is on the two tasks that are more important than any others in managing your hard disk efficiently: setting up your filing system, and periodically backing up your files—both to protect yourself against loss of data if your hard disk is inadvertently erased or damaged, and to clear out old files you no longer use regularly.

WHAT'S IN THIS QUICK REFERENCE

This quick reference to managing your hard disk doesn't cover the basics of using DOS; it assumes that you know what DOS is and how to use its commands. Rather, it focuses on the commands and techniques that let you take advantage of the hard disk's capacity and speed. Most of the material is taken from two other Microsoft Press books, *Running MS-DOS* and *Supercharging MS-DOS*; the information is selected and edited to concentrate the most relevant parts of DOS in this smaller, more convenient format.

- Part 1, "How a Hard Disk Works," describes how a hard disk stores information and how DOS finds the files it needs.

- Part 2, "Preparing Your Hard Disk," shows you how to use the Fdisk, Format, and Copy commands to identify the hard disk to DOS, prepare it for use, and copy the DOS files to it.

- Part 3, "Configuring DOS for Your Hard Disk," describes the configuration commands you should include in the file named CONFIG.SYS to make best use of your hard disk. It also includes some other techniques you can use to tailor your system to the hard disk.

- Part 4, "Working with Directories," describes the commands you use to set up your filing system and tell DOS where you keep your command and data files.

- Part 5, "Working with Files," describes the DOS commands you use to manage your files, emphasizing those that let you deal with the large number of files the hard disk can hold.

- Part 6, "Backing Up Your Hard Disk," describes the commands you use to back up and restore files between your hard disk and archival storage.

- Part 7, "Maintaining Your Hard Disk," suggests some things you can do to keep your hard disk running trouble-free.

WHAT TO TYPE AND WHEN

This quick reference uses the following conventions to distinguish what you do from how your computer responds:

- Hands-on examples are shown in different type, on separate lines, just as you would see them on your display. The characters you type are shaded. For example:

  ```
  C>path
  PATH=C:\;C:\DOS;C:\WORD;C:\EXCEL
  ```

- Occasionally, similar information appears in the text. In these instances, the interaction between you and the computer is printed in italics to distinguish it from the surrounding text. For example:

  If you type *path* to display the command path, but no command path is defined, DOS responds *No path*.

- The names of keys are shown in angle brackets (< >) to distinguish them from characters that you type; <Ctrl-Break>, for example, means hold down the Ctrl key and press the Break key.

- The examples show the system prompt as C>, as in the first example above. Your display will be different if the current drive isn't drive C, or if you have defined your own system prompt. Whenever you see C>, assume that it refers to the system prompt.

- Many commands include parameters that let you specify a drive letter, a file, or another variable. These parameters are shown in angle brackets to show that they represent a variable entry. When a parameter must be entered exactly, it is shown in the form you must use. For example:

  ```
  path <pathname> ;
  ```

  The word *path* and the semicolon are required and must be entered as shown. <pathname> represents the path name of a directory that you must type.

PART 1

How a Hard Disk Works

Information is stored on a disk much as music or video is recorded on magnetic tape. A brief description of how a hard disk is organized and how DOS uses it can help you understand the commands you use to manage it.

TYPES OF HARD DISK

Hard disks come in a variety of sizes and shapes. Most common is the internal drive, which is installed inside the system unit of your computer, usually beneath or beside the diskette drive. Several other types are available:

- Another type of hard drive, a hard disk on a card, fits inside the system unit but is mounted on a printed circuit card that plugs into a socket on the main circuit board, rather than adjacent to the diskette drive.

- An external drive is housed in its own case and sits beside the system unit. It is connected to the computer by a cable through which data passes and usually has its own power cord.

- Some hard disk drives, both internal and external, have removable cartridges that you can store and exchange just as you do diskettes.

All these hard disk drives operate much the same way; regardless of the type you have, you use the same techniques and commands to manage it.

Note: One type of disk drive, called the Bernoulli Box, has the capacity and speed of a hard disk but is really a special type of diskette sealed in a removable cartridge. Although you generally treat it just as you would a hard disk, there are a few special considerations; if you use a Bernoulli Box, check its documentation for any exceptions to the information in this book.

INSIDE A HARD DISK

A hard disk of the sort shown in Figure 1-1 contains two or more thin metal platters, 3.5 or 5.25 inches in diameter, stacked on a central axis, or spindle. A separate arm holds a series of read/write heads, one for each surface of each platter. An electric motor turns the spindle, rotating the platters so that they move past the heads.

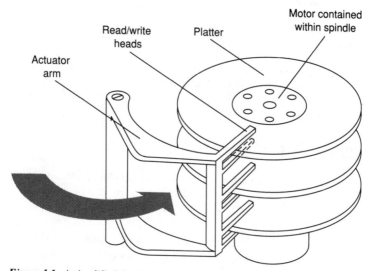

Figure 1-1. *A simplified drawing of the inside of a hard disk.*

The platters are coated with a magnetic material, similar to the coating on audio and video tape, so that information can be read from (played back) or written to (recorded on) the disk. This entire assembly, including the motor and the recording heads, is sealed in an airtight case.

Two factors give a hard disk greater storage capacity than a diskette:

- A hard disk drive contains more than one magnetically coated disk.

- Data can be recorded much more densely because the drive unit is enclosed in an airtight enclosure, the platters and magnetic coating are more finely machined, and the disks spin faster.

The storage capacity of diskettes used on MS-DOS computers ranges from 160 KB to 1.44 MB (although some less common units can store 6 MB or more). Typical hard disk capacities range from 10 MB to 70 MB, with 20 MB to 30 MB the most frequently used sizes. Much larger units are becoming more common; optional hard disks for the IBM PS/2 Model 80, for example, can hold as much as 314 MB, and third-party manufacturers offer drives for IBM-compatible computers with capacities as high as 760 MB.

SIDES, TRACKS, AND SECTORS

Just as on a diskette, data is stored on the platters of a hard disk in narrow concentric circles called tracks. Each track is divided into wedge-shaped segments called sectors; a sector holds 512 bytes. Each platter, of course, has two sides. These sides, tracks, and sectors are physical portions of the hard disk.

Figure 1-2 shows how tracks and sectors are laid out on one side of a hard disk platter.

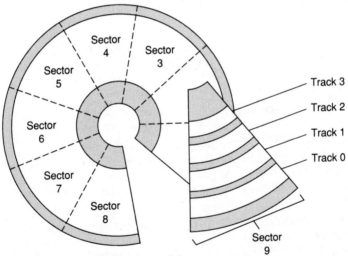

Figure 1-2. Tracks and sectors on a disk.

For simplicity, the illustration shows only four tracks, each divided into nine sectors. A hard disk has more tracks than this, and each track is divided into more sectors. The exact number of tracks and sectors varies, depending on the hard disk's capacity.

When DOS formats a hard disk, it numbers each side, track, and sector. When DOS stores a file on the disk, it stores the side, track, and sector numbers of the beginning of a file in the file's directory entry. The Directory command doesn't display this information, but DOS can find any sector on a disk by its side, track, and sector numbers, just as you can find any seat in a stadium or a theater by its section, row, and seat numbers.

But in most cases you don't have to deal with these platters and sides and tracks and sectors; true, they're part of the hard disk drive, but with rare exception all you need be concerned about is drive letters, path names, and file names.

Note: DOS occasionally uses the term *cylinder* when referring to a disk (for example, in responses to the Fdisk and Format commands). A cylinder is all the tracks with the same number on each side of each platter. If a hard disk has three platters, for example, cylinder 5 consists of the "stack" formed by the six tracks numbered 5 on the upper and lower surfaces of the three platters.

INSTALLING A HARD DISK

If the hard disk comes as part of the computer system, the dealer should install the hard disk, prepare it, format it, and—if you buy DOS at the same time—install DOS on it. The service personnel at most stores are professionals; they'll install the drive quickly and correctly, and test it to make sure it works.

If there's an extra charge for this service, either pay the price or go to a dealer who doesn't charge for it. If the dealer won't install the drive or won't guarantee the system, find one who will.

If you're adding a hard disk to your computer, you'll have to take the system unit in so they can install the drive. Again, if the dealer won't install it for you or will install it but won't guarantee the work, find a dealer who will.

But if you can't resist a low price for a hard disk drive from a mail-order house (or if a friend gives you one), either you'll have to find a computer service company that will install it for you or you'll have to install it yourself.

Installing the drive isn't especially difficult, if you have some experience with hand tools and if the directions that come with the drive are both clear and accurate. You'll probably need just one or two screwdrivers that match the screws used to attach the computer's case and hold in the disk drive—usually a medium-sized straight-slot and a #2 Phillips.

But the instructions that come with do-it-yourself drives probably won't include much detail because a drive can be put in so many different computers, and a mistake can be costly; the drive most likely isn't guaranteed against damage during installation, and poking around inside your computer probably voids its warranty too.

Unless you've installed a hard disk drive before—successfully— you're better off paying a professional to do it.

PART 2

Preparing Your Hard Disk

Preparing a hard disk for use means more than just formatting it as you would a diskette. In many cases, this preparation is done for you by the dealer or by the computer support person at your company. If you bought the computer from a dealer and discover that the hard disk isn't prepared, you should be able to take it back to the store and have someone there do it.

If you bought your computer by mail order, however, or if going back to the store isn't convenient, this part of the quick reference shows you how to prepare the hard disk and install DOS on it.

FINDING OUT IF YOUR HARD DISK IS READY TO USE

Sometimes the dealer not only prepares the hard disk, but—if you bought a copy of DOS at the same time—installs DOS so that the system is ready to run. To check how much preparation was done on your system, try to start the system from the hard disk by opening the latch on drive A and turning the system on.

If DOS displays the system prompt, the hard disk has been prepared and DOS has been installed; you can skip the rest of this part. If the system doesn't start, you must perform one or more of the following steps:

1. Identify the hard disk to DOS with the Fdisk command.
2. Format the hard disk with the Format command.
3. Copy the DOS system files from the system diskette to the hard disk with the Copy command.

The procedure that follows shows you how to determine what must be done and how to do it.

7

In the Fdisk procedures that follow, you'll encounter yet another term that DOS uses to refer to disk storage: *partition.* You saw in Part 1 that *side, track,* and *sector* are terms that refer to physical portions of the recording surfaces; their sizes are fixed by the design of the hard disk drive itself. A partition, however, is a portion of a hard disk that DOS (or some other operating system) treats as a single unit. The size of a partition can vary, depending on how you tell the Fdisk command to divide the disk.

DOS recognizes two types of partition. The *primary partition* is the system disk; DOS starts from it, and it can be no larger than 32 MB. The *extended partition* is the remainder of the hard disk; it can be any size, although if it's larger than 32 MB you use the Fdisk command to tell DOS to treat the extended partition as more than one disk drive, each of which can be no larger than 32 MB.

It's also possible to define a partition on a hard disk for use by an operating system other than DOS, but that isn't covered in this book.

IDENTIFYING THE HARD DISK TO DOS—FDISK

The procedure that follows shows you how to prepare your hard disk so that DOS can be started from it and only DOS can use it; it covers the IBM PS/2 series, the IBM Personal Computer AT and XT, and computers compatible with these models. The instructions make some assumptions about your hard disk and how you want to define it; see the documentation that came with DOS and your computer if:

- You have a different computer.

- Your hard disk is larger than 32 MB and you're not using 3.3 or a later version of DOS.

- Your hard disk is larger than 64 MB.

- You want to run both DOS and another operating system from your hard disk.

- You don't want to make the primary partition as large as possible.

- You want to tell DOS to treat the extended partition as more than one drive.

The following steps include instructions for creating more than one partition on your hard disk if your hard disk holds more than 32 MB.

You can do this only with versions of DOS beginning with 3.3; earlier versions do not allow more than a single DOS partition.

USING FDISK

The Fdisk command starts the Fdisk program, which helps you set up your hard disk for the first time or change the way DOS uses it. Fdisk is called a menu-driven program because it displays a series of screens from which you choose, much as you choose from a restaurant menu. Each choice you make causes Fdisk to display another menu, and so the procedure continues until you finish preparing your hard disk.

The Fdisk command has no parameters.

To use Fdisk to identify your hard disk to DOS:

1. Put the DOS system diskette in drive A (the lefthand or upper diskette drive) and turn the system on or restart it by pressing Ctrl-Alt-Del. DOS might prompt you for the correct date and time:

   ```
   Current date is Tue 1-01-1980
   Enter new date (mm-dd-yy): _
   ```

   If you don't see this prompt, skip to step 4.

2. If DOS displays the correct date, just press Enter. Otherwise, type today's date in numeric form, using the date format DOS displays in its *Enter new date* request. (In the United States, for example, you would enter October 16, 1988 as *10-16-88*.) Press the Enter key after you type the date. DOS prompts you for the time:

   ```
   Current time is 0:01:30.00
   Enter new time: _
   ```

   The current time DOS displays will differ, depending on how long your system has been on.

3. If DOS displays the correct time, just press Enter. Otherwise, type the current time, using a 24-hour clock. (For example, you would enter 2:30 P.M. as *14:30*.) Press the Enter key after you enter the time. Now DOS displays its opening message and the system prompt, which tells you that it is ready for you to enter a command:

   ```
   The IBM Personal Computer DOS
   Version 3.30 (C)Copyright International ....
               (C)Copyright Microsoft Corp ...

   A>_
   ```

4. Type the Fdisk command:

```
A>fdisk
```

DOS fills the screen with the first menu for the Fdisk command:

```
IBM Personal Computer
Fixed Disk Setup Program Version 3.30
 (C)Copyright IBM Corporation 1983,1987


FDISK Options


Current Fixed Disk Drive: 1


Choose one of the following:

    1. Create DOS partition
    2. Change Active Partition
    3. Delete DOS partition
    4. Display Partition Information


Enter Choice: [1]


Press ESC to return to DOS
```

(If you have more than one hard disk, Fdisk displays a fifth menu option, *Select Next Fixed Disk Drive*. Disregard it.)

5. Press the Enter key (this selects item 1). Fdisk displays another menu:

```
Create DOS Partition


Current Fixed Disk Drive: 1


    1. Create Primary DOS partition
    2. Create Extended DOS partition


Enter choice: [1]


Press ESC to return to FDISK Options
```

6. Press the Enter key to choose option 1. If the hard disk has already been prepared by your dealer or someone else, Fdisk responds *Primary DOS partition already exists* and *Press ESC to return to FDISK Options*. Press Esc once to return to the Fdisk menu, then press Esc again to return to DOS. Go on to the heading "Formatting the Hard Disk." If the hard disk hasn't been prepared, Fdisk responds:

```
Create Primary DOS Partition


Current Fixed Disk Drive: 1
```

```
Do you wish to use the maximum size
for a DOS partition and make the DOS
partition active (Y/N).........? [Y]
```

```
Press ESC to return to FDISK Options
```

The primary DOS partition is the one DOS starts from, and can
be as large as 32 MB. As mentioned at the beginning of this
section, these instructions show how to create a primary partition of the maximum size; press Enter to select Y (yes). DOS
responds:

```
System will now restart
```

```
Insert DOS diskette in drive A:
Press any key when ready...
```

7. The DOS system diskette is already in drive A, so press any
   key. DOS is restarted and again displays the date prompt. Set
   the date and time again, as you did in steps 2 and 3, if necessary. If your hard disk is 32 MB or less, go on to the heading
   "Formatting the Hard Disk."

8. If your hard disk is larger than 32 MB, you must identify the remainder of your disk space to DOS. To do this, type the Fdisk
   command again:

```
A>fdisk
```

Fdisk displays the same screen of options it did in step 4.

9. Again, press the Enter key to select item 1 (*Create DOS partition*). Fdisk displays the same screen of options it did in step 5.

10. This time, type *2* to choose *Create Extended DOS Partition* and
    press Enter. Fdisk shows a display like this:

```
Create Extended DOS Partition

Current Fixed Disk Drive: 1

Partition Status  Type   Start  End Size
  C: 1        A    PRI DOS    0  731  732

Total disk space is  979 cylinders.
Maximum space available for partition
is  531 cylinders.

Enter partition size..........: [ 531]

Press ESC to return to FDISK options.
```

The partition size Fdisk displays is the amount of remaining space on the hard disk. Press Enter to devote all of it to the extended DOS partition. Fdisk responds with the message *Extended DOS partition created.*

11. Press Esc. Fdisk displays a screen like this:

```
Create Logical DOS Drive(s)


No logical drives defined


Total partition size is  531 cylinders.


Maximum space available for logical
drive is  531 cylinders.


Enter logical drive size........: [531]


Press ESC to return to FDISK Options
```

Fdisk is asking you how to divide this space into one or more logical drives (*logical* because any drive you define acts just like an independent disk drive, even though it's not a physically separate piece of equipment). Press Enter to assign all remaining disk space to one logical drive, then press Esc twice to end the Fdisk program.

Press any key to restart your system and, if necessary, enter the correct time and date as you did earlier.

FORMATTING THE HARD DISK

Warning: Formatting the hard disk erases any files that may be stored on it, so follow this procedure only if the hard disk has not yet been formatted or if you don't need any of the files stored on it.

1. Type the Format command:

```
A>format c: /s /v
```

DOS displays a message before starting to format the disk, giving you a chance to cancel the command because formatting erases any files on the disk:

```
WARNING, ALL DATA ON NON-REMOVABLE DISK
DRIVE C: WILL BE LOST!
Proceed with format (Y/N)?
```

2. Press y and then press Enter. The light on the hard disk goes on; DOS displays a constantly changing message telling you the

head and cylinder number being formatted, and prepares the hard disk for use. This takes several minutes. When DOS finishes, it responds:

```
Format complete
System transferred

Volume label (11 characters, ENTER for none)?
```

DOS is waiting for you to type an identifying name, or volume label, for the disk. The volume label is displayed each time you display the directory of the drive; you can change this name at any time with the Label command.

3. Type any name of up to 11 characters and press the Enter key. This completes formatting your primary DOS partition. DOS responds by telling you how the disk space is allocated and then displays the system prompt.

4. If you devoted your entire hard disk to DOS, go on to the heading "Copying the DOS Files to the Hard Disk." If your hard disk is larger than 32 MB, format each of the logical drives you assigned to the extended DOS partition, this time without transferring the DOS system files. For example, if you assigned the entire extended partition to drive D, you would type:

```
A>format d: /v
```

Be sure to give each logical drive a different volume label.

COPYING THE DOS FILES TO THE HARD DISK

With the DOS system diskette still in drive A, create a directory especially for DOS on drive C:

```
A>md c:\dos
```

Now copy the DOS files from the system diskette in drive A to your DOS directory. Type:

```
A>copy *.* c:\dos
```

DOS displays the names of the files as it copies them. When all the files have been copied, DOS again displays the system prompt. Because you formatted the hard disk with the /S option of the Format command, the file COMMAND.COM is now in both the root directory and your new DOS directory. It only needs to be in the root directory, so delete it from the directory named \DOS by typing:

```
A>erase c:\dos\command.com
```

Remove the DOS system diskette from drive A and store safely.

If you're using 3.5-inch diskettes, you're done; go on to the next paragraph. If you're using 5.25-inch diskettes, you must copy the remaining DOS files. Insert the other DOS diskette in drive A and repeat the preceding command (*copy *.* c:\dos*).

Finally, you need to tell DOS where to find its command files whenever you start it from drive C. Do this by creating a special file named AUTOEXEC.BAT, which DOS looks for whenever it starts up. Type the following, entering ^Z by holding down the key labeled Ctrl and pressing Z. If you make a mistake before pressing Enter at the end of a line, backspace to the error and correct it. If you notice an error after you press Enter, press the keys labeled Ctrl and Break and try again; if you notice an error after pressing Ctrl and Z, retype the whole thing:

```
A>copy con c:\autoexec.bat
path c:\dos
^Z
```

DOS responds *1 File(s) copied*. You're done.

TESTING THE HARD DISK

To make sure the procedures were successful, restart DOS from the hard disk. Open the door on drive A so that DOS won't try to start from that drive, then restart DOS by pressing Ctrl-Alt-Del (hold down the keys marked Ctrl and Alt, and press the key marked Del).

If all went well, the system prompt is C> rather than A>, showing you that the hard disk is the current drive.

If DOS doesn't restart properly, press Ctrl-Alt-Del again, making sure that you are holding both the Ctrl and Alt keys down while you press the Del key. If DOS still doesn't restart properly, put the DOS system diskette back in drive A, close the latch, and press Ctrl-Alt-Del to restart the system from the system diskette. Go back to the heading "Identifying the Hard Disk to DOS" and repeat the procedure.

A ONE-TIME PROCESS

Unless you decide to change the size of the partitions on your hard disk or you start using another operating system, you only need to use the Fdisk command when you first prepare your hard disk. Upgrading to a new version of DOS is a much simpler procedure, described under the heading "Installing a New Version of DOS on Your Hard Disk" in Part 7, "Maintaining Your Hard Disk."

PART 3

Configuring DOS for Your Hard Disk

A hard disk has a greater capacity than a diskette and operates much more quickly. To make the best use of its size and speed, however, you have to tailor DOS to handle more files and move data more quickly. You do this with a file named CONFIG.SYS, which contains configuration commands—commands that tell DOS what devices are attached to your system and that control how DOS uses your computer's memory.

CONFIG.SYS is a text file that you create with a text editor, such as Edlin, or with a word processor that lets you store a file with no formatting codes or other special characters; it must be in the root directory of the system disk. Each time DOS starts, it carries out the commands in CONFIG.SYS.

To make the most efficient use of your hard disk, your CONFIG.SYS file should include the Buffers command, which specifies how many disk buffers DOS allocates, and the Files command, which specifies how many files DOS can use at the same time. Depending on how your system is set up, you might also need to include the Lastdrive command, which sets the highest drive letter that DOS recognizes.

If you use a RAM disk—a simulated disk drive that uses part of your computer's memory—there must also be a Device configuration command in CONFIG.SYS to name the program file that controls the RAM disk; depending on which version of DOS you're using, this file could be named VDISK.SYS or RAMDRIVE.SYS.

If there is no file named CONFIG.SYS in the root directory of the system disk, DOS assumes values for each of these configuration parameters.

USING THE BUFFERS
CONFIGURATION COMMAND

A buffer is an area of memory that DOS uses to hold data that's being moved back and forth between disks and programs. Up to a certain point, having more buffers lets DOS operate more quickly by speeding the flow of data between disks and memory. The Buffers configuration command specifies how many buffers DOS uses.

The optimum number of buffers depends on several factors:

- The types of disk drives you use. A small increase in the number of buffers speeds hard disk operations.

- The size of your computer's memory. Each buffer reduces available memory by 528 bytes, so a large number of buffers might cause some programs to run more slowly because they have less memory to work in.

- The types of programs you use. Increasing the number of buffers can speed up certain types of programs—database programs, for example—that perform a lot of random disk access (jump from place to place in a data file).

- The number and levels of subdirectories in your file structure. If you have many subdirectories organized in several levels, increasing the number of buffers can significantly speed disk operations.

A hard disk requires at least 3 buffers. A database program might require 10 to 20 buffers for optimum performance. If you use a large number of subdirectories, DOS might need 10 to 25 buffers. Some programs may suggest or require a minimum number of buffers.

Specifying too many buffers, however, can slow down the system, because DOS might then be able to read a record from disk faster than it could search through all the buffers. Finding the optimum number of buffers might require some experimentation. After changing the number of buffers, use your system for a while and note its performance, then change the number of buffers and repeat your observations.

DOS uses the following number of buffers unless you specify otherwise with a Buffers command in CONFIG.SYS:

2   If your system is an IBM PC, a PC/XT, or a compatible computer

3   If your system includes a diskette drive with a capacity greater than 360 KB; for example, the IBM PC/AT

5	If your system has more than 128 KB of memory (DOS version 3.3 or later)
10	If your system has more than 256 KB of memory (DOS version 3.3 or later)
15	If your system has more than 512 KB of memory (DOS version 3.3 or later)

The Buffers configuration command has one parameter:

`buffers=<number>`

<number> is the number of buffers. Valid numbers are 1 through 99 in versions of DOS numbered 3.2 and earlier, and 2 through 255 in version 3.3.

Buffers Example

Suppose you have a 30 MB hard disk and 640 KB of memory, and you regularly use a database program. This type of configuration would benefit from 20 buffers; put the following command in CONFIG.SYS:

`buffers=20`

NEED TO USE MORE FILES? THE FILES CONFIGURATION COMMAND

DOS keeps track of file usage in two ways, depending on how an application program is designed. One of these ways, typical of applications written for DOS version 2.0 and later, relies on a DOS-assigned number called a handle to keep track of each open file and device on the system. The Files configuration command sets the maximum number of such handle-based files and devices that DOS can use at the same time.

If you don't specify otherwise, DOS assumes eight available handles, five of which are preassigned for use by DOS. This number is sufficient for most uses, but some programs—especially database programs—must have more than eight handles open at one time. The manual that comes with your programs should tell you if you need to increase this value; some programs even include an installation utility that puts the proper Files configuration command in CONFIG.SYS for you.

The Files configuration command has one parameter:

`files=<number>`

<number> specifies the maximum number of files that DOS can use at the same time. <number> can be from 8 through 255; if you don't specify <number>, DOS assumes 8. Each additional open file above 8 increases the memory used by DOS by 48 bytes.

Files Example

Suppose that a program you use needs as many as 20 files available at the same time; put the following command in CONFIG.SYS:

`files=20`

NEED MORE DRIVE LETTERS? THE LASTDRIVE CONFIGURA- TION COMMAND

Unless you specify otherwise, DOS recognizes drive letters A through E. Five drive letters might seem more than adequate, but it isn't hard to use them up. For example, suppose you have one diskette drive; DOS assumes it's both A and B. If your hard disk is 40 MB, you must define it as drives C and D because DOS cannot use a drive larger than 32 MB. Then you define a RAM disk, which is drive E. You're out of drive letters.

Now what if you want to define a directory as a separate disk with the Substitute command, or you add another hard disk to your system? Or suppose your system is attached to a network, and you must define drives to use the network directories. You need more drive letters.

The Lastdrive configuration command lets you specify the highest drive letter that DOS recognizes. You can use it to specify a maximum of 26 drives.

The Lastdrive configuration command has one parameter:

`lastdrive=<letter>`

<letter> specifies the highest drive letter that DOS recognizes. It can be any letter from A through Z. If <letter> represents fewer than the number of disk drives physically attached to the computer, DOS ignores the Lastdrive command.

Lastdrive Example

To allow 10 drive letters, include the following command in
CONFIG.SYS:

```
lastdrive=j
```

USING A RAM DISK

A RAM disk, or virtual disk, is an area of memory that you tell DOS
to use as if it were another disk drive attached to your computer. It's
called a RAM disk because the computer's memory is called RAM,
for Random Access Memory. You can use a RAM disk just as you
would use a real disk drive: You can create files and subdirectories on
it, copy files to and from it, even run the Check Disk (chkdsk) command on it. Because it has no moving parts, a RAM disk is much
faster than a real disk drive. Using a RAM disk not only saves time, it
also saves wear and tear on your real disk drives.

You don't need any additional hardware to install a RAM disk, just a
program that persuades DOS to treat a portion of memory as a disk
drive—a disk drive that happens to be very fast. Some versions of
DOS include such a program; it's called VDISK.SYS starting with
version 3 of the IBM release, and RAMDRIVE.SYS starting with version 3.2 of other releases. (VDISK stands for virtual disk, another
name for a RAM disk.) Most add-on memory cards also include a
RAM-disk program. Even if you don't have a RAM-disk program, you
might want to skim this topic just to see what the advantages of a
RAM disk are.

To use a RAM disk, you copy the program and data files you need
from a real disk drive to the RAM disk, then copy the data files back
to the real disk after you finish with them. Copying the data files back
is particularly important, because the revised version of a file is stored
only in memory when you use a RAM disk, and the contents of
memory are lost whenever you turn off your computer or restart DOS.

Despite its speed, there is a cost to using a RAM disk: Because the
memory used by a RAM disk isn't available to DOS or other programs, your system must have enough memory to run DOS and all
your application programs without the memory you assign to the
RAM disk. If, however, your computer is equipped with extended
memory above 1 MB (available for the IBM PC/AT or IBM PS/2
models 50 and 60, or compatible computers), or if it contains an
expanded-memory board that increases memory in accordance with
the Lotus/Intel/Microsoft Expanded Memory Specification, you can

tell DOS to use this additional memory for your RAM disk, while
leaving your computer's more conventional memory space for programs to use.

Making a RAM Disk Work for You

To take advantage of the speed of the RAM disk, you copy the data
files, batch files, and programs you'll be working with to the RAM
disk. Be sure to leave enough unused space on the RAM disk to allow
for the increased size of files that you edit, plus any backup files that
your application programs create automatically.

To simplify setting up the RAM disk, you can write a batch file (or
batch files) to copy to the RAM disk the files and programs you need.
If you consistently use the same setup, put the commands in
AUTOEXEC.BAT so that the RAM disk will be ready to use when
DOS first displays the system prompt.

If you use a RAM disk regularly, a couple of cautions are in order:

- Back up your work frequently to a real disk. If the power fails
  or you forget you're using a RAM disk and turn off the system,
  all the work you did using the RAM disk is lost.

- Leave room for enough directory entries. Using all the directory
  entries keeps you from storing any more files, just as if you had
  filled the disk. Remember, most word processors and text edi-
  tors create backup files, so you need up to twice as many directory entries as the number of files you work on. Some
  application programs also create temporary files, which they
  delete before returning to DOS; each temporary file also requires a directory entry.

- A directory entry requires only 32 bytes, so you can safely
  specify 64 directory entries. That takes up only 2 KB of the
  RAM disk and should avoid the problem of filling the disk. If
  you'll be working with many small files or using several different application programs, specify at least 128 directory entries.

Defining a RAM Disk

You define a RAM disk by putting a Device configuration command
that names the RAM-disk program (named either VDISK.SYS or
RAMDRIVE.SYS) in CONFIG.SYS and then restarting the system.
The command parameters specify the capacity, sector size, and maximum number of directory entries of the RAM disk.

The RAM-disk program assigns the next available drive letter to the RAM disk. For example, if you have two diskette drives (A and B), the RAM disk would be drive C; if you have one diskette drive and a hard disk (drive C), the RAM disk would be drive D.

Note: If you have a non-DOS RAM-disk program, such as SUPERDRV.COM from AST Research, Inc., you may have to assign a drive letter to your RAM disk; other details of the command description that follows might also be different. Check the manual that came with your RAM-disk program for differences.

The Device command to define a RAM disk has the following parameters.

For IBM versions of DOS numbered 3.0 and later:

`device=vdisk.sys <size> <sector> <directory> /E`

For MS-DOS versions 3.2 and later:

`device=ramdrive.sys <size> <sector> <directory> /E /A`

VDISK.SYS or RAMDRIVE.SYS is the name of the program that simulates the disk drive in memory. If the program isn't in the root directory of the system disk, you must include its drive letter and path name.

<size> is the size, in kilobytes, of the RAM disk. The minimum is 1 if your program is named VDISK.SYS and 16 if it is named RAMDRIVE.SYS. The maximum size is the total amount of memory available on your computer. If you omit <size> or specify an incorrect value, DOS sets <size> to 64.

<sector> is the size, in bytes, of each sector on the RAM disk. You can specify 128, 256, or 512 with either VDISK.SYS or RAMDRIVE.SYS; you can also specify 1024 with RAMDRIVE.SYS. If you omit <sector> or specify an incorrect value, DOS sets <sector> to 128.

<directory> is the number of directory entries allowed in the root directory of the virtual disk. You can specify from 2 through 512 with VDISK.SYS; you can specify from 3 through 1024 with RAMDRIVE.SYS. Each directory takes up 32 bytes of the RAM disk. If you omit <directory> or specify an incorrect value, DOS sets <directory> to 64.

/E can be used only with a computer that contains extended memory above 1 MB. It tells DOS to use this extended memory for the virtual disk, leaving the maximum amount of memory available for programs. You can use /E only with the IBM PC/AT, IBM PS/2 models

50 and 60, and computers compatible with those models. If you use /E, you cannot use /A.

/A can be used with a computer that contains an expanded memory board that meets the Lotus/Intel/Microsoft Expanded Memory Specification. It tells DOS to use this expanded memory for the virtual disk, leaving the maximum amount of memory available for programs. You can specify /A only with RAMDRIVE.SYS (included with non-IBM releases of DOS). If you use /A, you cannot use /E.

Example of Using a RAM Disk

Assume that your RAM-disk program is stored in the directory \DOS on drive C. To define a 100 KB RAM disk with 256-byte sectors and room for 75 directory entries, you would include one of the following Device commands in CONFIG.SYS:

```
device=c:\dos\vdisk.sys 100 256 75
```

or

```
device=c:\dos\ramdrive.sys 100 256 75
```

Now suppose that you wanted to run your word-processing program using the RAM disk. First, you would put one or more Copy commands in AUTOEXEC.BAT to copy the word-processing program to the RAM disk (drive D). Then you could either: change the current disk to the RAM disk and start the word processor; or write a batch file to copy the document file (or files) to be edited to the RAM disk, start the word processor, then copy the document files back to the real disk when you're through editing them. You could call such a batch file WP.BAT, and put the following commands in it. (The line numbers are for reference only.)

```
1. @echo off
2. cd \wp
3. copy %1 d:
4. d:
5. word
6. c:
7. copy d:%1
8. erase d:%1
9. cd \
```

To edit a file named REPORT.DOC using the RAM disk, you would type *wp report.doc*; lines 3 and 7 of the batch file take care of copying the original files from the hard disk to the RAM disk and copying the changed files back from the RAM disk to the hard disk.

By including a wildcard character (* or ?) as part of the file name you specify, you could use this same batch file to edit a set of files with similar names or extensions. For example, to work with all the files whose names start with LET and whose extension is DOC, you would type *wp let*.doc*. Notice, however, that this would copy all the files that match the file name *let*.doc* to the RAM disk and then copy them back to the real disk, whether or not you had changed them.

MAKING YOUR HARD DISK LARGER

You can't really make your hard disk larger, of course, but a data-compression program can make the disk seem larger by reducing the amount of disk space required to store a file. Such programs—called *file-compression programs*—reduce the size of a file by using various techniques, such as replacing a series of identical characters with a special (shorter) code. Some file-compression programs work only with particular application programs; SQZ!, for example, works only with Lotus 1-2-3. Other file-compression programs, such as Cubit, work with any application program.

Because file-compression programs actually change a file before storing it on disk, the compressed file must be expanded to its original content whenever it is copied from disk to the computer's memory. You can't use a compressed file with any program unless you first expand it. Some compression programs automatically compress and expand files whenever DOS copies them between memory and disk; others require you to compress and expand files with a command before and after you use them. In either case, moving a file to or from a disk takes longer.

Using a file-compression program sacrifices file-access speed to gain disk space; the tradeoff can be particularly obvious with larger files (25 KB or more). Whether the tradeoff is worth your while is something you must decide.

Using Disk Caches

Hard disks are much faster than diskettes, but programs are available to make them work even faster. Two common techniques rely on either a *disk cache* or an *in-memory index*. Where the file-compression programs trade off disk-access time for disk storage space, these speedup programs trade off available computer memory for disk-access time.

A cache, like a buffer, is an area of memory used to hold data read from a disk. But a cache is much larger than a typical DOS buffer, and the disk-cache program keeps track of what's in the cache and where it was stored on the disk. When DOS asks for more data from the disk, the cache program checks whether the data is already in the cache. If the data is there, the cache program returns the data to DOS almost immediately, avoiding the need to read the data from the disk.

Depending on the size of the cache, the techniques that the disk-cache program uses to fill it, and the types of programs you use, the apparent increase in disk speed can be dramatic. Remember, though, that the memory used by the cache isn't available to DOS or other programs. If you use several memory-resident popup programs, such as Sidekick and others, you may find that you have to give up one or two of them in order to use the cache program.

The in-memory index requires only the use of the Fastopen command, added to DOS in version 3.3.

Speeding Up File Access with the Fastopen Command

Each time DOS needs a file, it must search for the subdirectory that contains the file, then search the directory entries for the file itself. On a hard disk with hundreds or thousands of files, all this searching takes time.

The Fastopen command tells DOS to keep an in-memory index of the locations of subdirectories and files as it uses them; the next time it's asked for a file or subdirectory, DOS checks this index before it searches the disk. If the location of the file or subdirectory is in memory, DOS can go directly to it instead of having to search for it on the disk.

If you tend to use the same files or directories over and over, the Fastopen command can make DOS visibly faster. Like a disk cache, Fastopen requires memory that becomes unavailable for other uses. But because only the locations of the files and directories—not their contents—are kept in memory, the amount of memory used is much smaller than the amount required for a disk cache.

The Fastopen command works only with hard disks; it has two parameters:

```
fastopen <drive>=<files>
```

<drive> is the drive letter, followed by a colon, of the hard disk whose files and subdirectories you want DOS to keep track of.

<files> is the number of files and subdirectories whose locations DOS is to keep in memory. <files> must be separated from <drive> by an equal sign. If you don't specify <files>, DOS keeps track of the location of the last 34 files and subdirectories (the last 10 in non-IBM releases of DOS).

Fastopen Example

If you wanted DOS to keep track of the last 75 files and subdirectories used on drive C, you would type the following command:

```
C>fastopen c:=75
```

Note: You can enter the Fastopen command only once during a session with DOS. You cannot, for example, start a session with the command *fastopen c:=25* and later decide that you want DOS to keep track of more files. To change the number of files, you must restart your computer.

If you routinely want to use the Fastopen command with the same number of files, put the command in AUTOEXEC.BAT.

TAILORING YOUR STARTUP PROCEDURE WITH AUTOEXEC.BAT

In addition to putting configuration commands in CONFIG.SYS, you can tailor your system's operation by specifying a series of commands to be carried out or programs to be run each time you start your system. You do this by putting the commands in a file named AUTOEXEC.BAT in the root directory of the system disk. Like CONFIG.SYS, AUTOEXEC.BAT is a text file; it must be in the root directory of the system disk. Each time DOS starts, it carries out the commands in AUTOEXEC.BAT.

At a minimum, you'll probably want to include the required commands to set the correct date and time. If your system doesn't have a clock/calendar, put Date and Time commands in AUTOEXEC.BAT so that DOS will prompt you to enter the date and time. If your system does have a clock/calendar, it probably came with a program that sets the clock that DOS uses from the clock/calendar; put the command that runs this program in AUTOEXEC.BAT. (You needn't bother with this if you're using version 3.3, because it automatically sets the DOS clock if your system has a clock/calendar.)

To make best use of your hard disk, you may want to put other commands in AUTOEXEC.BAT. For example, if you use programs such as a disk cache, data compressor, or automatic backup, putting the commands that start these programs in AUTOEXEC.BAT means you won't have to type the commands each time you start the system. You can also use AUTOEXEC.BAT to tailor your system, help DOS find program files, and help you keep track of your directories with the Path and Prompt commands described in Part 4. Here, for example, is a simple AUTOEXEC.BAT file that tells DOS where to find external DOS commands (in the \DOS directory) and application programs (in the \WORD and \EXCEL directories), clears the screen, and changes the prompt to display the current directory:

```
@echo off
path=c:\;c:\dos;c:\word;c:\excel
cls
prompt [$p]
```

PART 4

Working with Directories

In most ways, you treat a hard disk as if it were a large diskette, using the DOS directory commands to create, change, and remove directories, and the DOS file commands to copy, erase, rename, and otherwise work with your files. You can use the Volume and Label commands with a hard disk, but two diskette commands—Diskcopy and Diskcomp—don't work with the hard disk because they are specifically designed to work only with entire diskettes.

The DOS file system is layered, or *hierarchical;* a directory can contain not only files but also other directories, which are called *subdirectories.* These subdirectories, in turn, can contain either files or more subdirectories, creating a structure of directories within directories. Because a drawing of the resulting file organization looks something like an upside-down tree, it is sometimes referred to as a tree-structured file system.

When DOS formats a disk, it creates a top-level directory called the *root directory,* which it identifies with a single backslash character, \. Thus, for example, the root directory of drive C is identified as C:\.

The root directory holds a limited number of entries; depending on the capacity of the disk, the number varies from 112 on a 360 KB diskette to at least 512 on a hard disk. As discussed later, however, it's a good idea not to put a lot of unnecessary files in the root directory of your hard disk; limiting the root directory to a few files helps you keep track of the hundreds or thousands of files that will eventually be stored on the disk.

Unlike the root directory, a subdirectory can hold any number of files and other directories. A subdirectory is simply a file that holds directory entries, and there is no arbitrary limit on the size of a file, so there is no arbitrary limit on how many entries a subdirectory can contain. Thus, any number of the files in the root directory can be subdirectories, that, in turn, can contain any number of files themselves. Disk capacity is the only real limit on the number of subdirectories and files you can create.

Within this potential labyrinth of subdirectories, DOS identifies each file by its path name: the file name itself, preceded by the list of directory names, starting with the root, that leads to the directory containing the file. Each directory name is separated from the others by a backslash. For example, suppose the root directory contained a directory named WP, which contained a directory named CLIENTS, which contained a file named 12–10LET.DOC; its path name would be C:\WP\CLIENTS\12–10LET.DOC

Because DOS keeps track of files by their path and file names, you can give files in different directories the same name and extension. The following two path names, for example, guide DOS to entirely different files:

```
C:\WP\CLIENTS\12-10LET.DOC
C:\WP\LEGAL\12-10LET.DOC
```

SETTING UP YOUR DIRECTORIES

Your directory structure isn't just a place to store application programs and data files; it should provide a logical framework for your work with the computer. You might organize your directories by program type (word processor, spreadsheet, and so forth), by department (such as Marketing, Engineering, and Administration), by some combination of these, or in any other way that matches the way you use the computer. The structure should feel natural, and you should be able to find a file without searching through several similar-sounding directories.

Figure 4-1 shows some root-level subdirectories that you could use to contain your most frequently used programs and batch files. You might choose different directory names, but these are the types of files you want to be readily available, yet easily distinguished. All these directories should be in the command path you define with the Path command.

Directory	Contains
\DOS	All DOS files (and nothing but DOS files); this makes it easy to find a DOS file or change to a new DOS version.
\BATCH	Batch files you use frequently, plus any other files they may require.
\PGM	Utility programs, programs used by your batch files, and application programs that don't require a separate directory.
\WP	The word-processing program you use. Document files would be in subdirectories. You might give this directory the same name as the program (if you use Microsoft Word, for example, you would probably name the directory \WORD).
\SPREAD	The spreadsheet program you use. Spreadsheet files would be in subdirectories. You might give this directory the same name as the program (if you use Microsoft Excel, for example, you would probably name the directory \EXCEL).
\DB	The database program you use. Database files would be in subdirectories. You might give this directory the same name as the program (if you use RBase System V, for example, you would probably name the directory \RBFILES).

Figure 4-1. Suggested subdirectories for programs and batch files

CREATING AND REMOVING DIRECTORIES

There is no correct number of directories to use for your files. If you have to search through dozens or hundreds of files to find the one you need, you probably have too few directories; if it's hard to remember just where you stored a file, or if you find yourself frequently typing really long path names, you may have too many directories. You're looking for a balance that lets you remember where files are stored and find a particular file fairly quickly.

Before you start creating directories, do some planning. Consider the programs you use and how you use the computer. If you were setting up a paper file system for the same jobs you'll be doing with the computer, how would you label the drawers on the filing cabinet? What sorts of major categories would you set up inside the drawers? Sketch a directory structure that best seems to match the work you do.

You'll find that such planning really is valuable. Your directory structure will certainly evolve as you add new programs or clients, or as you find that a directory is getting too crowded and it's time to split it, but wholesale change in a directory structure that has accumulated several hundred files is tedious—you can't move the files; you must copy them to their new directory, then erase them from the old one.

You need only two DOS commands to manage your filing system:

- Make Directory (mkdir, abbreviated md), which creates a subdirectory.
- Remove Directory (rmdir, abbreviated rd), which deletes an empty subdirectory.

Creating a New Directory—MD

The Make Directory command creates a new directory. You can abbreviate the command *md*. Because the Assign, Join, and Substitute commands can mask the real identity of directories, you shouldn't create new directories when any of those commands are in effect. The Make Directory command has one parameter:

```
md <path>
```

<path> is the path name of the directory to be created. If <path> begins with a backslash (\), the path starts at the root directory; if <path> doesn't begin with a backslash, the path starts at the current directory. There is no limit to the number of levels of subdirectories, but the maximum length of a path name from the root directory is 63 characters.

Make Directory Examples

In the following examples, assume that the current directory is C:\.

To create a subdirectory named WP in the current directory of the current drive:

```
C>md wp
```

To create a subdirectory named WP in the directory named \MKT of the disk in drive A:

```
C>md a:\mkt\wp
```

Removing a Directory—RD

The Remove Directory command (rmdir or rd) removes a directory. You can abbreviate the command *rd*. Because the Assign, Join, and Substitute commands can mask the actual subdirectory names, you shouldn't remove a directory when any of these commands are in effect. The Remove Directory command has one parameter:

`rmdir <pathname>`

<pathname> is the path to the directory that is to be removed. The directory must be empty. You cannot remove the current directory or the root directory.

Remove Directory Examples

In the following examples, assume that the current directory is C:\.

To remove the directory \MKT on the disk in the current drive:

`C>rd mkt`

To remove the directory \MKT\WP on the disk in the current drive:

`C>rd \mkt\wp`

To remove the directory \LETTERS on the disk in drive A:

`C>rd a:\letters`

KEEPING TRACK OF WHERE YOU ARE

When you have created a directory structure, you'll want to move around from directory to directory, doing work here and there. As files accumulate, so do directories, and pretty soon you could have a problem keeping track of where you are in the directory structure, and find yourself jumping around in order to use different programs.

DOS gives you some commands to make sense of this and simplify your work:

- The Change Directory command (chdir, abbreviated cd) changes or displays the current directory.
- The Prompt command lets you tell DOS to display the current directory as part of the system prompt.
- The Path command tells DOS where to find program files that aren't in the current directory.
- The Append command tells DOS where to find data files that aren't in the current directory.

The last two commands let you use your programs and data files no matter where you are in the directory structure.

Changing and Displaying the Current Directory—CD

The Change Directory command changes or displays the current directory. You can abbreviate it *cd*. The Change Directory command has one parameter:

```
cd <drive><pathname>
```

<drive> is the drive letter, followed by a colon, of the drive whose current directory is to be displayed or changed. If you omit <drive>, DOS assumes the current drive.

<pathname> is the path name of the directory that is to become the current directory. If you omit <pathname>, DOS displays the current directory of <drive>. If you're changing to a subdirectory of the current directory, you can omit the current directory from <pathname>.

If you omit both <drive> and <pathname>, DOS displays the current directory of the disk in the current drive.

Change Directory Examples

Assume that the current directory is C:\WORD.

To display the current directory of the current drive:

```
C>cd
C:\WORD
```

To change the current directory in the current drive to \WORD\MKT:

```
C>cd mkt
```

To change the current directory in the current drive to the root directory (\):

```
C>cd \
```

(The backslash moves you immediately to the root directory from any directory.)

To change the current directory on the disk in drive A to \LETTERS:

```
C>cd a:\letters
```

To display the current directory on the disk in drive A:

```
C>cd a:
A:\LETTERS
```

Using the .. Entry to Move Around the Directories

When you use the Dir command to list a directory that contains subdirectories, the subdirectories are identified as <DIR>. For example:

```
Volume in drive C is MYDISK
 Directory of  C:\
DOS             <DIR>       3-11-88   12:11p
WORD            <DIR>       3-26-88    8:14a
```

When you list the contents of the subdirectory, the display begins as follows:

```
Volume in drive C is MYDISK
 Directory of  C:\DOS
.               <DIR>       3-11-88   12:11a
..              <DIR>       3-11-88   12:11a
XCOPY    EXE    11247       3-17-87   12:00p
ANSI     SYS     1678       3-17-87   12:00p
```

The .. entry in such a directory listing represents the directory immediately above the current directory, and you can use it to move quickly around a directory structure. For example, if you're in the directory \WORD\MKT\MEMOS:

- Type *cd* .. to change to \WORD\MKT.
- Type *cd* ..\ .. to change to \WORD.
- Type *cd* ..*letters* to change to \WORD\MKT\LETTERS.

Making the System Prompt Show the Current Directory

As your directory structure grows, it gets harder and harder to remember where you are. Instead of typing a Change Directory command to display the current directory, you can tell DOS to keep the name of the current directory on display.

The system prompt normally consists of the current drive letter followed by a greater-than sign (usually C>). The Prompt command lets you define the system prompt to show any of several items of system information, such as the current directory, current drive, time, or date, as well as any other words or symbols the computer can display.

The Prompt command has one parameter:

`prompt <string>`

<string> is a string that defines the new prompt. It can contain any printable character, plus any number of two-character codes to include

certain system values in the prompt. Each code begins with a dollar sign; the following table shows the second character of each code and the system value it represents:

Code	Information displayed
t	The time (in the form hh:mm:ss.hh)
d	The date (in the form mm-dd-yyyy, preceded by the day of the week)
p	Current directory of the current drive
v	DOS version number
n	Current drive
g	A greater-than sign (>)
l	A less-than sign (<)
b	A vertical bar (¦)
q	An equal sign (=)
h	A backspace (which erases the previous character)
e	An Escape character
_	(underscore) Start a new line
$	A dollar sign ($)

If any other character follows the $, DOS ignores both characters.

The string ng, for example, defines the standard system prompt: $n displays the current drive letter, and $g displays the greater-than sign. Because the prompt can include the Escape character, you can use the Prompt command to control the display if the ANSI.SYS console-control program is being used. (CONFIG.SYS must include the command device=ansi.sys.)

If you enter a Prompt command with no parameters, DOS resets the system prompt to the standard version.

Prompt Examples

In the following examples the current directory is C:\DOS. Each prompt-definition string ends with a space to move the cursor beyond the end of the system prompt. (This is shown in the example of the new prompt that follows each Prompt command.)

To define the system prompt as the current directory enclosed in brackets:

```
C>prompt [$p]
[C:\DOS] _
```

To define the system prompt as the current directory enclosed in brackets, followed by a space, the word *Command*, and a colon:

```
C>prompt [$p] Command:
[C:\DOS] Command: _
```

To define the system prompt as the date, time, and current directory, each on a separate line:

```
C>prompt $d$_$t$_$p
Sun 10-16-1988
16:07:31.56
C:\DOS _
```

To define the system prompt as the time, followed by six backspaces (to erase the hundredths of a second and seconds), a space, and the current directory enclosed in brackets:

```
C>prompt $t$h$h$h$h$h$h [$p]
16:07 [C:\DOS] _
```

Telling DOS Where to Find Command Files—Path

The Path command tells DOS where to search for a program file—a file whose extension is COM, EXE, or BAT—that isn't in the current directory. By defining a command path, you can use a program or an external DOS command no matter what the current directory is. Because you'll always want DOS to know where you have stored your programs, batch files, and external DOS command files, you should include a Path command in AUTOEXEC.BAT.

The Path command has three parameters:

```
path <drive><pathname> ;
```

<drive> is the letter, followed by a colon, of the drive containing the disk on which you want DOS to look for command files.

<pathname> is the path to the directory that DOS should search for command files. You can enter a series of path names separated by semicolons.

If you type *path* followed by just a semicolon, DOS deletes any command path in effect.

If you type a Path command with no parameters (type just *path*), DOS displays the path names it currently searches for command files. If no path has been specified, DOS displays *No path*.

Path Examples

To define the command path as the directory named DOS in the root directory of the current drive:

```
C>path \DOS
```

To define the command path as the directories named \DOS, \WORD, and \BATCH on drive C:

`C>path c:\dos;c:\word;c:\batch`

Assume that the command path is defined as the directories in the preceding example. To display the command path:

`C>path`

DOS responds:

`PATH=C:\DOS;C:\WORD;C:\BATCH`

To delete the command path:

`C>path ;`

Telling DOS Where to Find Data Files—Append

If you're using version 3.3, you can use the Append command to tell DOS where to look for a data file that isn't in the current directory. Just as with the Path command, you can name one or more directories on any disk drive.

The Append command has three parameters:

`append <drive><path> ;`

<drive> is the letter, followed by a colon, of the drive with the disk that contains the data files (such as A:). If you omit <drive>, DOS looks in the directory specified by <path> on the current drive.

<path> is the path name of the directory that contains the data files.

You can specify several data paths in one command, separating them with semicolons.

If you type *append* followed by just a semicolon, DOS cancels any data path in effect.

If you type an Append command with no parameters (type just *append*), DOS displays the path names it currently searches for data files. If no data path has been specified, DOS displays *No append.*

For example, suppose you use a word-processing program stored in the directory \WORD; it uses several auxiliary program files whose extension is OVL, and some data files for a spelling checker and thesaurus whose extension is WP. The Path command only tells DOS how to find the main program file, whose extension is EXE. By typing *append \word*, you can tell DOS where to find these other files, too, letting you use the program from any directory.

Because the Append command masks the real location of a file, you should use it sparingly.

MOVING THE DOS FILES TO A DIRECTORY NAMED \DOS

Files have a tendency to collect in the root directory, sometimes by the hundreds, until you get a directory structure established. This makes it just as difficult to find a computer file as it would be to find a particular paper file if you tossed them all in the same drawer.

The only files that DOS insists be kept in the root directory are COMMAND.COM, CONFIG.SYS, and AUTOEXEC.BAT. Some application programs might also require files in the root directory; the documentation that came with the program should tell you, and the program itself may create the files when you install it. Reserving the root directory for nothing but files that must be there and subdirectories makes it much easier to use your hard disk.

If you have already stored your DOS files in a directory other than the root, skip to the topic "Creating, Changing, and Removing Directories." If the DOS files are in the root directory, it's worth the time to move them.

Note: The following procedure assumes that DOS has been installed on your hard disk. If it hasn't—if you still must start the system with the DOS diskette in drive A—turn to the heading "Installing a New Version of DOS on Your Hard Disk" in Part 7, "Maintaining Your Hard Disk" and follow the instructions there. When you finish, you can skip this topic because the DOS files will be in a directory named \DOS.

The following steps show you how to create a directory named \DOS, put the DOS files in it, and remove the DOS files from the root directory.

1. Create a directory named DOS in the root directory to contain the DOS files, then make that directory the current directory by typing the following Make Directory and Change Directory commands:

    ```
    C>md \dos
    C>cd \dos
    ```

2. Put the DOS diskette you use to start the system in drive A, and copy the DOS files:

    ```
    C>copy a:*.*
            22 File(s) copied
    ```

37

The number of files copied will be different if you're not using version 3.3 of IBM's release of DOS.

3. The file named COMMAND.COM must be in the root directory of the system disk, but you don't need it in C:\DOS. It's already in the root directory, so delete it from C:\DOS:

```
C>erase c:\dos\command.com
```

If you're using 3.5-inch diskettes, skip to step 5.

4. Put the other DOS diskette in drive A, and copy the DOS files it contains:

```
C>copy a:*.*
      31 File(s) copied
```

Again, the number of files copied will be different if you're not using version 3.3 of IBM's release of DOS.

5. So that you'll know which DOS files you can delete from the root directory, print a sorted listing of all the DOS files you copied to C:\DOS by piping the output of the Directory command to the Sort filter command, then redirecting the output to the printer:

```
C>dir | sort > prn
```

6. Now change the current directory to the root and print a copy of its sorted directory listing:

```
C>cd \
```

7. Take the two printed directory listings and mark off all files on the root directory listing that appear on both lists.

8. Erase all the files from the root directory that you marked off its directory list.

Now that you have moved the DOS files to a directory named \DOS, you have to do a bit of housekeeping to make sure that DOS knows where to find its files.

Changing CONFIG.SYS

If there is a file named CONFIG.SYS in the root directory of your hard disk, it may contain some Device commands that name certain DOS files.

If it does, you must change these commands so that they refer to the new location of the DOS files (C:\DOS), not the root directory (C:\).

Check CONFIG.SYS by displaying its contents with a Type command:

```
C>type config.sys
```

If DOS responds *File not found*, there is no file named CONFIG.SYS, so skip to the heading ''Adding \DOS to the Command Path.''

If DOS displays the contents of the file, check each line to see if it is a Device command that names a file, such as *device=c:\vdisk.sys*. If it is, use your text editor or word processor (if it lets you store a file with no formatting commands) to change each Device command so that it refers to \DOS, not the root directory.

For example, you would change the file named earlier in this paragraph to *device=c:\dos\vdisk.sys*.

Adding \DOS to the Command Path

Now you've got to use the Path command to tell DOS where to find its command files. You'll put this command in the file named AUTOEXEC.BAT.

First, check the contents of AUTOEXEC.BAT with the Type command:

```
C>type autoexec.bat
```

If DOS responds *File not found*, type the following to create the file with the Path command you need (press Ctrl-Z where you see ^Z):

```
C>copy con autoexec.bat
path c:\dos
^Z
    1 File(s) copied
C>_
```

If, in response to *type autoexec.bat*, DOS displays a series of commands, edit the file using a text editor or word processor. If there is no Path command, add the line *path c:\dos* to the file. If there is a Path command (such as *path c:* or *path c:\;c:\word*), add a semicolon and *c:\dos* to the end of the command and save the revised version of your AUTOEXEC.BAT file.

Testing the New DOS Directory

Double-check your work by typing *dir c:\command* to make sure the root directory contains COMMAND.COM, because DOS won't start without it. If it isn't there, put the DOS diskette you use to start the system in drive A and copy COMMAND.COM to the root directory.

Next, type *dir c:\dos* to make sure that \DOS contains the DOS files. If you're not sure you can recognize the DOS files, look for files named CHKDSK.COM, FORMAT.COM, FIND.EXE, or other familiar DOS command names. If the DOS files aren't there, copy them from the DOS diskettes to \DOS (steps 2 through 4 of the procedure).

Now it's time to make sure everything works. Open the latch on drive A and press Ctrl-Alt-Del to restart the system. DOS should start just as it did before. If it doesn't, the problem is most likely one of these:

- If the system displays *Non-system diskette. Insert system diskette and press any key.* and DOS doesn't display the system prompt, DOS hasn't been installed on the hard disk. Turn to the heading "Installing a New Version of DOS on Your Hard Disk" in Part 7, "Maintaining Your Hard Disk" and follow the instructions there.

- If the system displays *Bad or missing COMMAND.COM* and DOS doesn't display the system prompt, COMMAND.COM isn't in the root directory. Close the latch on drive A (so that DOS will start from the startup diskette) and press Ctrl-Alt-Del again. When DOS is running, copy COMMAND.COM from the DOS diskette you use to start the system to the root directory on the hard disk, and restart the system.

- If the system displays a message such as *Bad or missing VDISK.SYS*, but DOS does display the system prompt, or prompt for the date and time, a Device command in CONFIG.SYS probably still refers to the root directory instead of C:\DOS. Go back to the heading "Changing CONFIG.SYS" and follow the instructions there.

When DOS displays the system prompt, check the command path by typing a Path command with no parameters:

`C>path`

The command path that DOS displays should include C:\DOS (for example, PATH=C:\DOS or PATH=C:\;C:\WORD;C:\DOS). If DOS responds *No path* or the path doesn't include C:\DOS, go back and repeat the instructions beginning with "Adding \DOS to the Command Path."

If the root directory in your hard disk still contains application programs and data files, you should eventually move them to other directories. As you learn what the files are for and get more comfortable with the tree-structured filing system, you can create directories for them, copy them to the new directories, and delete them from the root directory.

CHANGING THE WAY DOS TREATS DRIVES AND DIRECTORIES

Warning: The Join and Substitute commands let you change the way DOS interprets drive letters. These commands restrict your use of other DOS commands, such as Backup, Restore, and Print, that deal with disks and files. Use these commands sparingly, and check the descriptions of the other disk and file commands in your DOS manual to make certain you understand the restrictions. The Substitute and Join commands cannot be used on a network.

Treating a Disk Drive As If It Were a Directory—Join

The Join command equates a disk in one drive to a directory on a second drive; DOS treats the entire directory structure of the disk in the joined drive as if it were contained in the directory on the disk in the drive to which it is joined. If you use an application program that insists on storing data files only on the program disk, the Join command lets you circumvent the restriction and store your data files on another disk.

Once you have joined a drive to a directory on another drive, you can't use its drive letter in any DOS command. Because the Join command masks the actual type of disk drive from DOS, you shouldn't use the Backup, Diskcopy, or Restore commands when a join is in effect, nor should you enter an Assign or Substitute command that involves a joined drive. If you want to use one of these commands, or need to use the drive, delete the Join with the /D parameter. You cannot use the Join command with a network drive.

The Join command has three parameters:

```
join <drive1> <drive2>\<directory> /D
```

<drive1> is the drive that is to be joined to a directory on the second drive. The complete directory structure of the drive is joined, starting at the root, regardless of the current directory.

<drive2>\<directory> is the drive and directory to which <drive1> is to be joined. <directory> must be in the root directory of <drive2>. If <directory> doesn't exist, the Join command creates it; if <directory> does exist, it must not contain any files. You cannot join to the root directory of <drive2>.

/D disconnects any join involving <drive1>.

If you type a Join command with no parameters (type just *join*), DOS displays all joins in effect.

Join Examples

Suppose you use a word processor that stores document files only on the program disk, but you want to use files on the disk in drive B. The following command tells DOS to treat drive B as if it were a directory named DOCS in the root directory of the disk in drive C:

```
C>join b: c:\docs
```

If the directory \DOCS doesn't exist on drive C, DOS creates it. If it does exist and isn't empty, DOS displays *Directory not empty*.

Assume that you joined drive A to C:\DRIVEA and drive B to C:\DRIVEB. To display the joins in effect, type a Join command with no parameters:

```
C>join
```

DOS displays the joins in effect:

```
A: => C:\DRIVEA
B: => C:\DRIVEB
```

If no joins are in effect, DOS displays nothing.

To delete any joins affecting drive B (such as in the first example):

```
C>join b: /d
```

Treating a Directory As If It Were a Disk Drive—Substitute

The Substitute command equates a drive letter with the path name of a directory. This lets you store application programs and data files in directories even if the application program doesn't permit the use of path names.

If your directory structure has several levels, you can also use the Substitute command to save keystrokes by replacing a long path name with a drive letter.

If you substitute a drive letter for a directory, then want to substitute the same drive letter for a different directory, you must first delete the original substitution.

Because the Substitute command masks the actual type of disk drive from DOS, you shouldn't use the Assign, Backup, Diskcomp, Diskcopy, Fdisk, Format, Join, Label, or Restore commands when a substitution is in effect. Because the Substitute command can mask the true directory structure, you should avoid using the Change Directory, Make Directory, Remove Directory, and Path commands when a substitution is in effect. If you want to use one of these commands, delete the substitution. You can't use the Substitute command with a network drive.

```
subst <drive> <pathname> /D
```

<drive> is the letter, followed by a colon, of the drive to be substituted for <pathname>. <drive> cannot be the current drive. If you specify <drive>, you must also specify <pathname>.

<pathname> is the path to the subdirectory to be substituted for <drive>; it must begin at the root directory (start with \). If you include a drive letter in <pathname>, it must be different from <drive>. You must specify at least a backslash to name the root directory.

/D deletes a substitution, returning the drive letter to its original meaning.

If you enter the Substitute command with no parameters (type just *subst*), DOS displays all substitutions in effect.

Substitute Examples

Suppose you're using a word processor that doesn't allow path names when you name a file, but does let you specify a different drive; you want to keep the word-processing program in a directory named \WP and some word-processing files in a directory named \MKT\WP, all on the hard disk in drive C. The following Substitute command tells DOS to treat the directory C:\MKT\WP as if it were drive E:

```
C>subst e: \mkt\wp
```

If you want to use several directories for different types of word-processing files, enter a Substitute command for each directory using different drive letters. If you need drive letters beyond E, put a Last-drive configuration command in CONFIG.SYS to tell DOS the highest drive letter you will use.

Suppose your spreadsheet program is in C:\SPREAD and the spreadsheets are in subdirectories of that directory. Budgets are in a directory named C:\SPREAD\BUDGETS, and budget forecasts are in C:\SPREAD\BUDGETS\FORECAST. If you have to type that path name more than once, you could make your life easier by telling DOS to treat that directory as if it were drive F:

```
C>subst f: \spread\budgets\forecast
```

Suppose you had made the substitutions of the first two examples. The following command displays any substitutions in effect:

```
C>subst
E: => C:\MKT\WP
F: => C:\SPREAD\BUDGETS\FORECAST
```

The following command deletes the substitution created by the first example:

```
C>subst e: /d
```

PART 5

Working with Files

The sheer number of files on a fixed disk means that you'll probably spend much less time swapping diskettes, but a lot more time finding the files you need, clearing out unused files, moving files around, copying files to other disks, and generally keeping house.

This part focuses on some techniques and commands that can help you manage your filing system, showing you how to:

- Name your files to keep track of them better.
- Protect your files against inadvertent change or deletion.
- Combine files and copy to and from devices with the Copy command.
- Copy entire directory structures with the Xcopy and Replace commands.
- Copy only changed files or only those that have changed since a certain date with the Xcopy command.
- Replace only files that already exist on the target disk or directory—or add only those that don't exist there—with the Replace command.
- Display and print the directory structure—with or without the names of all the files—with the Tree and Check Disk commands.
- Use two batch files—described at the end of this part—to move a file from one directory to another or to find a file anywhere on the disk.

NAMING YOUR FILES

Consistency in naming your files lets you manage them more easily. For example, if you always use an extension with file names but never with directory names, typing *dir *.* lets you display just the names of directories. If you use the extension LET for all files that contain letters, you can display the names of all such files by typing *dir *.let*.

Suppose you use the following convention to name files that contain letters:

- The first three characters identify the recipient.
- The next two characters identify the month (01 through 12).
- The next two characters identify the date (01 through 31).
- The extension is always LET.

TJW1112.LET, then, would be the name of a letter to someone whose initials are TJW, written (or last changed) November 12. So that the parts of the file name always begin at the same position, start the month or day with a zero if the number is less than 10: A letter to TJW written on March 8, for example, would be stored in TJW0308.LET.

This scheme lets you display the names of all files that contain letters by typing *dir *.let*, display the names of all letters written to TJW by typing *dir tjw **, or display the names of all letters written in July by typing *dir ???07**.

Special Extensions

The following table describes some extensions that have special meaning to DOS. These extensions either are created by DOS or cause DOS to assume that the file contains a particular type of program or data. You should avoid giving your files any of these extensions.

Extension	*Meaning to DOS*
BAK	Short for *Backup*. Contains an earlier version of a text file. Edlin (the DOS text editor) and many word processors automatically make a backup copy of a file and give it this extension.
BAS	Short for *BASIC*. Contains a program written in the BASIC programming language. You can't run this program by typing its name; you can run it only while using the BASIC language.
BAT	Short for *Batch*. Identifies a text file that you can create, which contains a set of DOS commands that are run when you type the name of the file.
COM	Short for *Command*. Identifies a command file that contains a program DOS runs when you type the file name.

(continued)

Extension	Meaning to DOS
CPI	Short for *Code Page Information*. Describes the characters that a device can use. Used beginning in DOS version 3.3.
EXE	Short for *Executable*. Like COM, identifies a command file that contains a program DOS runs when you type the file name.
INI	Short for *Initialize*. Describes how a program should start operating. Used by Microsoft Windows, Microsoft Word, and other programs.
PIF	Short for *Program Information File*. Describes how an application program works; used by Microsoft Windows.
SYS	Short for *System*. Identifies a file that can be used only by DOS.

Some application programs also use special extensions. For example, Microsoft Word, the Microsoft word processor, uses DOC to identify a document, BAK to identify a backup version of a document, and STY to identify a file that contains a style sheet of formatting specifications. You should avoid using any extensions that have special meaning for your application program; these extensions are usually listed in the program's manuals.

PREVENTING ACCIDENTAL CHANGES AND DELETIONS

If you're using version 3 of DOS, you can make a file read-only with the Attribute command; once you have done this, the file can't be changed or deleted until the read-only attribute is turned off. One inadvertent change or deletion could make you wish you had protected your files this way.

When used to control the read-only status of a file, the Attribute command has four parameters:

```
attrib +R -R <filename> /S
```

+R tells DOS to make <filename> read-only; that is, to deny all attempts to change or erase <filename>.

−R tells DOS to let <filename> be changed or erased.

<filename> is the name of the file whose read-only status is to be affected. If you enter the command with <filename> only, DOS displays the name of the file and, if the file is read-only, displays an R

to the left of the file name. You can check or change the read-only status of a set of files with similar names or extensions by using wild-card characters.

/S applies the Attribute command not only to the file or files specified by <filename> in the specified directory, but to all matching files in all subdirectories contained in the specified directory. You can specify /S only if you're using 3.3 or a later version of DOS.

It doesn't take long to protect the files that you change infrequently or not at all, or those that simply mustn't be changed accidentally. For example, if all the DOS files are in the directory named \DOS on drive C, you can make them all read-only by typing:

```
C>attrib +r \dos\*.*
```

To make the file CONTRACT.DOC in the current directory read-only, you would type:

```
C>attrib +r contract.doc
```

To allow CONTRACT.DOC to be changed, you would type:

```
C>attrib -r contract.doc
```

Note: If you're using 3.2 or a later version of DOS, you can also use the Attribute command to control a file's archive attribute, which is used by the Backup and Xcopy commands, and by non-DOS backup programs, to determine whether a file has been changed since it was last backed up. This use of the Attribute command is described in Part 6, "Backing Up Your Hard Disk."

COPYING FILES

Starting with version 3.2, DOS includes three commands you can use to copy files: Copy, which has been around since version 1, and the newcomers, Xcopy and Replace, added in version 3.2. Why three commands? Wouldn't one be enough?

Each command has its strengths—functions it performs more quickly than the others or, in some cases, functions the other two don't provide at all. The following descriptions of these three commands for copying files point out these differences.

The Copy Command

The Copy command copies one or more files or the output from a device to another file or to the input to a device. Only the contents of a file are copied; its read-only status and archive status are not.

Although the newer copy commands offer some options that the Copy command lacks, Copy still has an advantage and some capabilities not available with either the Xcopy or Replace command:

- The Copy command is built into the portion of DOS always in memory; DOS doesn't have to find and load a separate command file to carry out the command.

- Only the Copy command can copy to and from a device.

- Only the Copy command can combine several files into one.

The Copy command has eight parameters:

```
copy <source> /A /B +<source> <target> /A /B /V
```

<source> is the name of the file or device to be copied. You can use wildcard characters to copy a set of files with similar names or extensions. You can combine several source files into one target file by separating the source-file names with a plus sign (+)—if you don't specify <target>, the files are combined into the first source file in the series; otherwise, the files are combined into <target>.

<target> is the name of the file or device to which <source> is to be copied. If <source> is to be copied to the same directory on the same disk, <target> must be different from <source>. If you omit <target> and specify a source file on a different drive or in a different directory, the file is copied to a file with the same name in the current directory. You can specify just a drive letter, a path name, or a file name as <target>, with the following results:

Target	*Result*
Drive letter	The <source> file is copied to a file with the same name in the current directory of the specified drive.
Path name	The <source> file is copied to a file with the same name in the specified directory.
File name	The source file is copied to a file with the specified name in the current directory.

/A treats the preceding file in the Copy command (and all subsequent files until a /B is encountered) as an ASCII, or text file. The Copy command assumes you're copying an ASCII file when you combine files or when you copy a file to or from a device. The effect of /A depends on whether you specify it with <source> or <target>:

- <source> files are copied up to the first Ctrl-Z character. Any data that follows the first Ctrl-Z is not copied.

- DOS writes a Ctrl-Z (end-of-file) character at the end of <target>.

/B treats the preceding file in the Copy command (and all subsequent files until a /A is encountered) as a binary file. The effect of /B depends on whether you specify it with <source> or <target>:

- <source> files are copied in their entirety (the file size as recorded in the directory entry).

- DOS does not write a Ctrl-Z (end-of-file) character at the end of <target>.

/V verifies that the file was copied correctly. DOS turns verification on, copies the files, then turns verification off. This parameter is redundant if the DOS Verify option is on. Verification slows the copy procedure.

Examples of Using Copy to Make Copies of Files

To copy all files from the directory named \WORD\MKT\LETTERS on the disk in the current drive to the current directory on the disk in drive A:

```
C>copy \word\mkt\letters\*.* a:
```

To copy all files named FORECAST, regardless of extension, from the directory named \MKT on the disk in drive A to the current directory on the current drive, giving them the same name:

```
C>copy a:\mkt\forecast.*
```

To copy all the files whose extension is LET from the root directory of drive A to the directory named \WORD\LETTERS on the current drive, giving the copies the extension DOC:

```
C>copy a:\*.let \word\letters\*.doc
```

Examples of Using Copy to Combine Files

To combine the files named FCST.APR, FCST.MAY, and FCST.JUN in the current directory into a file named FCST.2Q in the current directory:

```
C>copy fcst.apr+fcst.may+fcst.jun fcst.2q
```

To add the files named FCST.MAY and FCST.JUN to the file named FCST.APR in the current directory:

```
C>copy fcst.apr+fcst.may+fcst.jun
```

To combine all the files with the extension DOC in the current directory, in the order in which their directory entries appear, into the file named TOTAL.DOC in the current directory:

```
C>copy *.doc total.doc
```

Note: When you use wildcard characters this way to combine source files into an existing target file, the original contents of the target file are lost—replaced by the contents of the combined source files. Although DOS does display the message *Content of destination lost before copy*, this message appears after the fact, when it's too late to stop the copy procedure. When combining files, verify that your target file either doesn't exist in the specified directory or that it doesn't contain information you want to keep. If it does exist, and you want other files added to it, use the plus sign between the names of the source files and specify the target file name first.

Examples of Using Copy to Copy to and from a Device

To copy the file REPORT.DOC to the display (CON):

```
C>copy report.doc con
```

The file is displayed. Using Copy in this way is the same as if you had used the Type command (*type report.doc*).

To copy from the keyboard (CON) to a file named REPORT.DOC in the current directory:

```
C>copy con report.doc
```

Type the lines you want in the file, pressing Enter to start each new line. To end the copy, press Ctrl-Z to mark the end of the file, then press Enter. If there is no file named REPORT.DOC, DOS creates it. Be careful, though: If there already is a file named REPORT.DOC in the current directory, DOS replaces it with what you typed; you could lose a valuable file this way, so be sure to choose the file name carefully when you copy from the console to a file.

To copy from the keyboard (CON) to the printer (PRN):

```
C>copy con prn
```

Type the lines to be printed. To print the lines, press Ctrl-Z to mark the end of the file, then press Enter.

The Xcopy Command

The Xcopy command, like the Copy command, makes copies of files, but it also lets you:

- Copy faster. When you copy several files, Xcopy is much quicker than Copy. Xcopy copies as many source files as will fit into memory at a time; Copy copies files one at a time.

- Copy an entire directory structure—all the subdirectories in the source directory, as well as all the files in them. If the corresponding directories don't exist on the target disk or directory, the Xcopy command creates them.

- Copy only files whose archive attribute is on—that is, files that have changed since they were last backed up.

- Copy only files that have changed since a particular date.

You can use the Xcopy command for all other routine copy operations except those specific to the Copy command—copying to and from devices, and combining files.

The Xcopy command has 10 parameters:

```
xcopy <source> <target> /A /M /D:<date> /E /P /S /V /W
```

<source> is the name of the file to be copied. You can use wildcard characters to copy a set of files with similar file names or extensions.

<target> specifies where <source> is to be copied. You can include any combination of drive letter, path name, and file name. The effect is the same as described for the Copy command.

/A copies only those files whose archive attribute is on and leaves the archive attribute unchanged.

/M copies only those files whose archive attribute is on, then turns off the archive attribute. This tells DOS (or any other program, such as a backup utility) that the file hasn't been changed since it was last backed up, and therefore doesn't need to be backed up.

/D:<date> copies only files whose date of creation or last change (as displayed by the Directory command) is the same or later than <date>.

/E creates subdirectories on <target> even if they're empty. /E has no effect if you don't also specify /S.

/P prompts you for confirmation before it copies each file specified in <source>.

/S applies the Xcopy command to all subdirectories contained in <source>. If you specify <source> as a drive letter or as the root directory of a disk, the Xcopy command copies all the directories and files from <source> to <target>. If you don't specify /S, the command copies only files in the source directory, as the Copy command does.

/V verifies that the copy of the file on <target> was stored correctly. This parameter can slow the operation of the Xcopy command somewhat, but it is good insurance if you're copying critical data and must be certain that it was copied correctly.

/W (for *wait*) prompts you to press a key before the Xcopy command begins. This gives you a chance to put in the correct diskette before starting to copy files.

Xcopy Examples

To copy all the files and subdirectories in the directory named \NEWFILES from the disk in the current drive to the current directory on the disk in drive A:

```
C>xcopy \newfiles a: /s
```

To copy the entire directory structure, starting with \LETTERS, on the disk in the current drive—including empty directories—to the current directory on the disk in drive A:

```
C>xcopy \letters a: /e /s
```

To copy all the files whose archive attribute is on from the directory \WORD\LETTERS on the disk in the current drive to the current directory of the disk in drive A, leaving the archive attribute unchanged:

```
C>xcopy \word\letters a: /a
```

To copy all the files whose archive attribute is on from the directory \WORD\LETTERS and all the subdirectories it contains on the disk in the current drive to the disk in drive A, turning off the archive attribute of the source files:

```
C>xcopy c:\word\letters a: /m /s
```

To copy all the files that have changed since April 27, 1988, from the directory \WORD\LETTERS and all the subdirectories that contain files on the disk in the current drive to the disk in drive A, prompting for verification before each copy:

```
C>xcopy c:\word\letters a: /d:4-27-88 /s /p
```

The Replace Command

The Replace command also makes copies of files. Like the Xcopy
command, it lets you copy an entire directory structure, and it uses all
of available memory to speed the copying of several files. It doesn't
let you base the copy on the archive attributes of the files or on
whether they have changed since a certain date, as the Xcopy command does, but it does let you base the copy files on whether or not
a source file exists on the target:

- You can copy only the source files that *do* exist on the target—
  in other words, replace files.

- Or you can copy only the source files that *don't* exist on the
  target—in other words, add files.

You can use the Replace command for all other routine copy operations except those specific to the Copy command—copying to and
from devices, and combining files.

The Replace command has seven parameters:

```
replace <source> <target> /A /S /R /P /W
```

<source> is the name of the file to be copied. You can use wildcard
characters to copy a set of files with similar file names or extensions.

<target> specifies where <source> is to be copied. You can include a
drive letter and a path name, but not a file name.

/A (for *add*) copies only the files specified in <source> that don't exist
in <target>. This lets you add files to <target> without replacing files
that already exist. If you don't specify /A, only the files specified in
<source> that exist on <target> are copied (replaced). If you specify
/A, you cannot specify /S.

/S applies the Replace command to all subdirectories contained in
<source>. If you specify <source> as the root directory of a disk, the
Replace command copies all the directories and files from <source>
to <target>. If you don't specify /S, the command copies only files in
the source directory, just as the Copy command does. If you specify
/S, you can't specify /A.

/R replaces files in <target> even if they are read-only.

/P prompts for confirmation before replacing or adding each file.

/W (for *wait*) prompts you to press a key before the Replace command
begins. This gives you a chance to put in the correct diskette before
starting to replace or add files.

Replace Examples

To replace all files whose extension is BAT in the directory named
\BATCH on the disk in the current drive with the files of the same
name in the current directory on the disk in drive A:

```
C>replace a:*.bat \batch
```

To add all files whose extension is BAT in the current directory on the
disk in drive A that do not exist in the directory named \BATCH on
the disk in the current drive:

```
C>replace a:*.bat \batch /a
```

To replace all files whose extension is BAT—even if they are read-
only—in every directory of the entire current disk with the files of
the same name in the current directory on the disk in drive A:

```
C>replace a:*.bat \ /r /s
```

Note: When you replace a read-only file, the new copy of the file is
also given the read-only attribute.

LISTING ALL THE FILES ON
THE DISK—TREE

The Tree command displays the path of each directory on a disk, followed by a list of the subdirectories contained in the directory. A
printed copy of this report can be helpful, especially if your filing
system has several levels, and it's not difficult to produce. Simply send
(redirect) the output of the Tree command to your printer with the >
redirection symbol (type *tree > prn*).

You can also tell the Tree command to display the name of each file
in each directory and, again, you can print a copy of the report. On a
fixed disk with several hundred files, however, this list could be several pages long. That's fine, if you really want to see where all your
files are stored, but it can be a bit much if all you're interested in is
the directory structure.

The Tree command has two parameters:

```
tree <drive> /F
```

<drive> is the letter, followed by a colon, of the drive that contains the
disk whose directory structure is to be displayed.

/F displays a list of the files in each directory.

Tree Examples

Assume that the root directory of the disk in drive C contains four subdirectories: DOS, MKT, MFG, and ENG; \MKT and \ENG, in turn, contain subdirectories named WP and 123. To print this directory structure:

```
C>tree > prn
```

DOS prints the following list:

```
DIRECTORY PATH LISTING FOR VOLUME MYDISK

Path: \DOS
Sub-directories:   None

Path: \MKT
Sub-directories:   WP
                   123

Path: \MKT\WP
Sub-directories:   None

Path: \MKT\123
Sub-directories:   None

Path: \MFG
Sub-directories:   None

Path: \ENG
Sub-directories:   WP
                   123

Path: \ENG\WP
Sub-directories:   None

Path: \ENG\123
Sub-directories:   None
```

To display the name of each file in each directory, as well as the directory structure, of the disk in the current drive, and to pause after each screenful:

```
C>tree /f | more
```

The files in the root directory are listed at the beginning of the display. Then comes the first of the remaining directories, followed by a list of any subdirectories it contains. Below this list are the names of the files in the directory itself.

The Tree command is in version 2.0 and later of the IBM releases of MS-DOS, and in version 3.2 and later of other releases. If you don't

have the Tree command, you can also use the Check Disk command
with the /V parameter to display a similar list of all the directories
and files on disk. You would type *chkdsk /v*. The Check Disk command displays the list of directories and files on the disk, followed
by its usual report on disk storage use and available memory.

SOME USEFUL BATCH FILES

Because there are so many files on a fixed disk, you'll find yourself
spending a lot more time housekeeping than you did with diskettes:
creating new directories, getting rid of directories you don't need any
more, rearranging files, copying files to diskettes, and generally tidy-
ing up your file structure so you can keep track of what you've got
and keep your disk from filling up. Batch files can be of great help
here. The ones described in this part show just two of the ways you
can use batch files to help with this housekeeping:

■ MOVE.BAT lets you move a file from one directory to another
  with a single command.

■ FINDFILE.BAT lets you locate a file no matter where it's
  stored on the disk.

Moving Files from One Directory
to Another

In a tree-structured filing system on a hard disk, you'll often want to
move a file from one directory to another. Doing this requires both a
Copy command to make a copy of the file in the new directory and an
Erase command to get rid of the old copy. The batch file MOVE.BAT
lets you move a file or a set of files with similar names or extensions
with a single command.

To create the file, use a text editor, such as Edlin, or use your word
processor if it lets you store a file with no formatting codes. Here are
the commands in MOVE.BAT. The line numbers are for reference
only:

```
1. @echo off
2. if not exist %1 goto quit
3. copy %1 %2
4. cls
5. echo The target directory contains the following files.
6. echo Please check for the file(s) you moved.
7. dir %2 /w ¦ more
```

```
 8. echo <Alt-255>
 9. echo If file(s) haven't been moved to target directory,
10. echo press Ctrl-Break to cancel. Otherwise:
11. pause
12. erase %1
13. echo <Alt-255>
14. echo File(s) moved and deleted from source.
15. goto end
16. :quit
17. echo File(s) not found
18. :end
```

(If you're familiar with batch files, note that you can speed up MOVE.BAT considerably by removing whichever comments and pauses you want.)

Here's how MOVE.BAT works, line by line:

- Line 1 turns echo off so that DOS won't clutter the screen by displaying the commands as it carries them out. If you're not using version 3.3 of DOS, don't include the @.

- Line 2 checks whether the file exists. If the file does not exist, it skips to the label *quit* in line 16.

- Line 3 copies the file (the first parameter, %1) from the current directory to the target directory (the second parameter, %2).

- Line 4 clears the screen.

- Lines 5 and 6 display a message.

- Line 7 displays a wide listing of the target directory, pausing after each screenful if the directory is large.

- Line 8 echoes a blank line. To enter line 8, type *echo*, press the spacebar, hold down the Alt key and type the number 255 on the number pad (don't use the numbers at the top of the keyboard), release the Alt key, and press Enter.

- Lines 9 and 10 display a message that gives you a chance to cancel the batch file before the Erase command is carried out.

- Line 11 waits for you to press a key before continuing; if you press Ctrl-Break, DOS asks you if you want to cancel the batch command by displaying the message *Terminate batch job (Y/N)?*

- Line 12 erases the file from its original directory.

- Lines 13 and 14 display a blank line and a message telling you the move has been completed.

- Line 15 skips to the label *end*.

- Lines 16 and 17 tell you if the file was not found.

■ Line 18 ends the batch file.

You have created a command with two parameters:

`move <source> <target>`

<source> is the name of the file to be moved (copied and then deleted). If you use wildcard characters in the file name, DOS displays the name of each file it copies. If you don't include a path name, DOS assumes the file or files are in the current directory. If you omit <target>, you must include a path name with <source> because DOS won't copy a file to itself.

<target> is the name of the directory to which the <source> files are to be copied. If you omit <target>, the file or files are copied to the current directory.

For example, assume that the current directory is \WORD\MKT. To move the file REPORT.DOC from the current directory to the directory named \WORD\LETTERS, you would type:

`C>move report.doc \word\letters`

or

`C>move report.doc ..\letters`

To move the file BUDGET.JAN from the directory \MKT\SPREAD to \EXCEL\MKT, you would type:

`C>move \mkt\spread\budget.jan \excel\mkt`

To move all the files in the directory named \MKT\WP to the current directory, you would type:

`C>move \mkt\wp\*.*`

Finding a File Anywhere on the Disk

It isn't hard to forget where you stored a file, especially if your fixed disk contains hundreds of files in a couple of dozen directories. FINDFILE.BAT simplifies the task of finding a file—at the expense of a bit of disk space—and usually finds the file in a few seconds.

FINDFILE.BAT takes advantage of the /V option of the Check Disk (chkdsk) command, which displays the name of each file. Instead of displaying this list of files, however, FINDFILE.BAT redirects it to a file named ALLFILES.DAT in a directory named \BATCH, then searches this file with the Find command for all file names that contain the string you specify.

ALLFILES.DAT isn't an especially large file. Its length depends on how many files are on the disk and how long the path names are; each directory entry averages between 30 and 40 bytes, so (estimating generously) on a 20 MB fixed disk with 1000 files, ALLFILES.DAT might be 40,000 bytes long. This isn't a bad price for the convenience.

Because the Check Disk command can take a minute or two on a large fixed disk with many files, FINDFILE.BAT doesn't run the Check Disk command unless you specify *new* as the second parameter or unless ALLFILES.DAT isn't in the directory named \BATCH. Except when you're doing something that requires changing many files, you won't have to tell FINDFILE.BAT to run Check Disk very often, so the search usually takes no more time than it takes DOS to search ALLFILES.DAT.

To create FINDFILE.BAT, use a text editor, such as Edlin, or use your word processor if it lets you store a file with no formatting codes. Here are the commands in FINDFILE.BAT; the line numbers are for reference only. Even though lines 7, 8, and 9 are shown on two lines here, type each as a single line. (Don't press Enter until you've typed the period at the end of each line.)

```
 1:   @echo off
 2:   cd \batch
 3:   if not "%1"=="" goto OK
 4: :INSTRUCT
 5:   echo <Alt-255>
 6:   echo COMMAND                RESULT
 7:   echo findfile STRING        Searches for files that
      contain STRING.
 8:   echo <Alt-255>              STRING must be entered in
      uppercase.
 9:   echo findfile STRING new    Forces a Chkdsk command
      before searching.
10:   goto END
11: :OK
12:   if "%2"=="" goto ONE_ PARM
13:   if "%2"=="new" goto CHKDSK
14:   goto INSTRUCT
15: :ONE_ PARM
16:   if exist \batch\allfiles.dat goto FIND_ IT
17: :CHKDSK
18:   echo Executing Check Disk command.
19:   chkdsk /v > \batch\allfiles.dat
20: :FIND_ IT
21:   find "%1" \batch\allfiles.dat
22: :END
```

Note: FINDFILE.BAT assumes that a directory named \BATCH already exists.

Here's how FINDFILE.BAT works, line by line:

■ Line 1 turns echo off. If you're not using version 3.3, don't include the @.

■ Line 2 changes the current directory to \BATCH (where FINDFILE.BAT is stored).

■ Line 3 skips the instructions if you specified at least one parameter.

■ Line 4 is a label that identifies the beginning of the commands that display instructions for using FINDFILE.BAT.

■ Line 5 echoes a blank line. Type *echo*, press the spacebar, hold down the Alt key and type the number 255 on the number pad (don't use the numbers at the top of the keyboard), release the Alt key, and press Enter.

■ Lines 6 through 9 display instructions for using FINDFILE.BAT.

■ Line 10 goes to the end of the batch file (from which it returns to DOS).

■ Line 11 is a label that identifies the beginning of the commands that check what was typed as a second parameter.

■ Line 12 skips to the label ONE_PARM if a second parameter wasn't typed.

■ Line 13 skips to the label CHKDSK if the second parameter typed is *new*.

■ Line 14 skips to the label INSTRUCT if the second parameter typed isn't *new*.

■ Line 15 is a label that identifies the command that checks whether there is a file named ALLFILES.DAT in the directory named \BATCH.

■ Line 16 skips to the label FIND_IT if there is a file named ALLFILES.DAT in the directory named \BATCH.

■ Line 17 identifies the beginning of the commands that run the Check Disk command.

■ Line 18 displays a message telling you that a Check Disk command is being run.

■ Line 19 is the Check Disk command with the /V parameter; the output is redirected to \BATCH\ALLFILES.DAT.

■ Line 20 is a label that identifies the Find command.

- Line 21 is the Find command that searches for the string typed as the first parameter.
- Line 22 is a label that identifies the end of the batch file.

Testing FINDFILE.BAT

You have created a command with two parameters:

```
findfile <STRING> new
```

<STRING> is the string of characters you want FINDFILE to search for. Because you're searching for a file, <STRING> should be part or all of a path name, file name, or extension. Because the output of the Check Disk command is uppercase, you must type the characters to search for in uppercase, too.

new tells the batch command to run the Check Disk command, creating a new copy of ALLFILES.DAT, before searching for <STRING>.

If you type the Findfile batch command with no parameters (type just *findfile*), it should display these instructions:

COMMAND	RESULT
findfile STRING	Searches for file names that contain STRING.
	STRING must be entered in uppercase.
findfile STRING new	Forces a Check Disk command before searching.

The first time you use it, FINDFILE.BAT runs the Check Disk command because there is no file named ALLFILES.DAT in the directory named \BATCH. To display the names of all files whose names contain EXE, you would type the following:

```
C>findfile EXE
```

FINDFILE.BAT would respond by telling you that it's running Check Disk, and then would display the names of the files it found. Because it uses the Find command, its response begins with a line that identifies the file searched (\BATCH\ALLFILES.DAT). The output would begin like this:

```
Executing Check Disk command.
----------- \batch\allfiles.dat
      C:\AUTOEXEC.BAT
      C:\DOS\ATTRIB.EXE
      C:\DOS\FIND.EXE
      C:\DOS\JOIN.EXE
      C:\DOS\SHARE.EXE
      C:\DOS\SORT.EXE
      C:\DOS\SUBST.EXE
      . . .
```

Your list would be different, and probably longer, but it should include these files (although not necessarily in the same order or directory).

Notice that, in addition to the files whose extension is EXE, the sample output also includes AUTOEXEC.BAT because it, too, contains the string EXE.

You could limit the output to just files with the extension EXE by including the period in the string to find:

```
C>findfile .EXE
```

This time there would be no message and the command would take much less time, because it wouldn't have to run the Check Disk command. And there would be no AUTOEXEC.BAT in the list of files. From now on, each search would be this fast until you specified *new* to force another Check Disk command or until you erased ALLFILES.DAT from \BATCH.

Whenever you have added or deleted enough files that you think you need a new list to search, add *new* as a second parameter following the search string.

PART 6

Backing Up Your Hard Disk

Making backup copies of the files on your hard disk is the most important way to protect yourself against the loss of valuable files. Even if you never mistakenly erase a file (or series of files), hardware and software failures beyond your control can happen. Take the time to back up your files periodically. It's like wearing a seat belt: the cheapest insurance available.

This part shows you how to use three DOS commands, Backup and Restore (which work together) and Xcopy, to back up files from your hard disk and restore them to the hard disk when you need them.

BACK UP YOUR PROGRAM DISKETTES

Even when treated with care, diskettes can still be mislaid or accidentally damaged. Making backup copies of your diskettes protects you if something goes wrong. The time it takes to make these copies could be one of your better investments.

Unless a program diskette is copy protected, make a copy of it before you ever use it—even though you plan to install the program on your hard disk. Store the original diskette in a safe place and use the copy. If something happens to the copy, make another copy from the original. Always keep the original stored safely.

It's easy to make a backup copy of a diskette. Keep your backup copies in a safe place and use your computer with the comforting thought that, should something unforeseen happen, you're protected.

DEVELOPING A BACKUP PROCEDURE

It could take a drawerful of diskettes to back up all the files on a hard disk: If your average file were 20,000 bytes long (a little more than 13 double-spaced typed pages), a full 20 MB hard disk would have more than 1000 files, and you would need almost 16 high-capacity (1.2 MB) diskettes to back them all up. If you were using 360 KB diskettes, you'd need nearly 60 of them.

But you don't have to back up all your files. You needn't back up program files, for example, because you've already got the original DOS and application-program diskettes (plus, of course, the backup diskettes you made). Some data files, such as a spelling dictionary, don't usually change, so it isn't necessary to back them up either.

How often you back up your other data files, such as word-processor documents and spreadsheets, depends on how often they change. For example, spreadsheets might change often while the budget is being prepared, but remain unchanged the rest of the year. The backup procedures you use depend on how you use your computer.

But no matter how you decide to back up your files, do it regularly. A system failure can happen, but if you're diligent about backing up your files, such a failure will be more of an inconvenience than a disaster. You never want to spend hours, days, or even weeks re-creating files that you could have backed up in a few minutes.

USING DOS TO BACK UP FILES

You could back up files from your hard disk to diskettes using the Copy command, but this is tedious, even if you automate the procedure with a batch file: The Copy command works with only one directory at a time, and it can't determine whether a file has been changed since it was last backed up. The temptation is to back up everything, which takes more time and uses more diskettes; the result often is to put off backing up.

DOS offers three commands much better suited to backing up files from a hard disk:

- ■ The Backup and Restore commands—which work together, as their names imply—were designed to let you back up only the files you want. You can use them to back up or restore files from many directories with a single command.

■ The Xcopy command—a general-purpose file-copying command—offers much the same capabilities as the Backup and
Restore commands.

Warning: Don't use the Backup or Restore command if you have
entered an Assign, Join, or Substitute command to alter the way DOS
interprets drive letters. Because these commands can mask the type of
drive, DOS could damage or delete the files you specify in the commands or other files on the disk.

Backing Up with the Backup Command

The Backup command makes a backup copy of files for protection
against damage to or other loss of files from the hard disk. Starting
with version 3.0 of the IBM release of DOS and version 3.1 of other
releases, you can back up files from any type of source disk (diskette
or hard disk) to any type of target disk; previous versions back up
only from a hard disk.

Rather than making an exact copy, as the Copy and Xcopy commands
do, the Backup command copies and stores files in a way that helps it
(and Restore) keep track of the disk and directory each file originally
came from.

Versions of DOS through 3.2 do this tracking by adding path and file
name information at the beginning of each file. Beginning with version 3.3, DOS collects the files it backs up in a single file named
BACKUP.00X (X is the DOS-assigned number of the backup disk);
path and file name information are in a separate file named
CONTROL.00X, also on the backup disk.

In all versions of DOS, the Restore command uses the path and file
name information to return each file, in its original form, to the disk
and directory from which it came. Because backup copies of files are
not identical to the originals, you must use the Restore command to
copy them back from the backup disk. Also, because the Backup and
Restore commands are not the same in all versions of DOS, you must
use the same version for backing up and restoring files.

Unless you're using version 3.3, you must format the target disk
before you back up files to it. Unless you use its /A (Add) option, the
Backup command erases any files on the target disk before making
the backup copies. It displays a warning message before erasing the
files, but, to be safe, be sure the backup diskette you use doesn't
contain any files you must keep.

If the files to be backed up require more than one diskette, DOS prompts you to insert another diskette; be sure to label these diskettes, because the Restore command requires them in the same order.

DOS displays the name of each file as it is backed up. If the target disk is a diskette, the backup files are stored in its root directory. If the target disk is a hard disk, the backup files are stored in a directory named \BACKUP.

The Backup command sets the following Errorlevel values:

0	Normal completion.
1	No files were found to back up.
2	Some files were not backed up because of a file-sharing conflict.
3	The backup process was terminated by the user pressing Ctrl-C.
4	The backup process was terminated by a system error.

You can check this value with the *errorlevel* option of the If batch command and use the result to determine which other commands in a batch file are carried out.

Note: If you back up files from a drive that is affected by an Assign, Substitute, or Join command, restoring the files with the Restore command can damage the directory structure of the disk to which the files are restored.

Although not all of the following options are available in every version of DOS, the Backup command can have up to nine parameters:

```
backup <source> <target> /S /M /A /D:<date> /T:<time> /
F /L:<logfile>
```

<source> specifies the file or files to be backed up. You can use wild-card characters to back up a set of files with similar names or extensions. You must specify at least a drive letter, followed by a colon, or a path name, or a file name; the following list shows what happens if you specify just one of these elements:

Drive letter	DOS backs up all files in the current directory of the disk in the specified drive.
Path name	DOS backs up all files in the specified directory on the current drive.
File name	DOS backs up the specified file from the current directory.

<target> is the letter of the drive, followed by a colon, that contains the backup disk.

/S backs up files in all subdirectories contained in the current or specified directory.

/M backs up only files that have been modified since they were last backed up.

/A adds the backup files to the backup disk rather than erasing the backup disk before starting the backup.

/D:<date> backs up only files that have been modified since the date specified in <date>. Specify <date> as you would for the Date command.

/T:<time> backs up all files that have changed since <time> on <date>. Enter <time> just as you would for the Time command. You can specify /T:<time> only in certain versions of DOS.

/F formats the target disk if it isn't already formatted. You can specify /F beginning with version 3.3 of DOS. The /F option uses the DOS Format command, so be certain the current command path includes the directory containing FORMAT.COM before you specify /F.

/L:<logfile> creates a log file on the source drive that contains the date and time of the backup, the path name and file name of each file that is backed up, and the number of the diskette on which each file is backed up. If a log file already exists, the backup information is added at the end, creating a history of backups for the source drive. If you don't specify a name for the log file, DOS names it BACKUP.LOG and stores it in the root directory of the source drive. You can specify /L:<logfile> only in certain versions of DOS.

Backup Examples

To back up all files whose extension is WKS from the current directory on the disk in the current drive to the disk in drive A:

```
C>backup c:*.wks a:
```

To back up all files whose extension is DOC from the directory named \WORD\MKT on the disk in the current drive to the disk in drive A:

```
C>backup c:\word\mkt\*.doc a:
```

To back up all files that have been modified since they were last backed up from the entire disk in the current drive (the root directory and all its subdirectories) to the disk in drive A:

```
C>backup c:\ a: /s /m
```

To back up all files whose extension is DOC from the current directory and all its subdirectories on the disk in the current drive to the disk in drive A, adding them to the backup disk:

```
C>backup c:*.doc a: /s /a
```

To back up all files whose extension is MSP that were changed on or after October 16, 1988, backing them up from the directory named \WIN on the disk in the current drive to the disk in drive A:

```
C>backup c:\win\*.msp a: /d:10-16-88
```

To back up all files from the current directory and all its subdirectories on the disk in the current drive that were changed on or after October 16, 1988 and have not been archived since then, to the disk in drive A, adding them to the backup disk:

```
C>backup c: a: /m /a /s /d:10-16-88
```

Restoring Files with the Restore Command

The Restore command copies files that were backed up with the Backup command from the backup disk to the disk you specify. You can restore files to a different drive (for example, back them up from drive C and restore them to drive D), but because the Backup command stores the full path name with each file, either the same directory structure must exist on the disk to which the files are restored or you must use the /S option to re-create the original directory structure. If you have a series of backup diskettes, DOS prompts you to enter them, as they are needed, in the same sequence as they were written by the BACKUP command.

The Restore command sets the following Errorlevel values:

0   Normal completion.

1   No files were found to restore.

2   Some files were not restored because of file-sharing conflict.

3   The restore process was terminated by the user pressing Ctrl-C.

4   The restore process was terminated by a system error.

You can check this value with the *errorlevel* option of the If batch command and use the result to determine which other commands in a batch file are carried out.

Warning: Trying to restore files that were backed up when an Assign, Substitute, or Join command was in effect can damage the directory structure of the disk.

Although not all of the following options are available in every version of DOS, the Restore command can have up to 10 parameters:

```
restore <source> <target> /S /P /B:<date> /A:<date> /M
/N /E:<time> /L:<time>
```

<source> specifies the drive that contains the backup disk from which files are to be restored.

<target> specifies the file to be restored. You can use wildcard characters to restore a set of files with similar names or extensions. If you don't specify a path name, files that belong in the current directory are restored. If you don't specify a drive letter, the files are restored to the disk in the current drive.

/S restores files in all subdirectories contained in the specified directory.

/P causes DOS to prompt for confirmation before restoring either a file that has changed since it was backed up or a file that is marked as a hidden or a read-only file. This lets you protect files that you have updated since you backed them up and avoid replacing the hidden system files (IBMBIO.COM and IBMDOS.COM, or IO.SYS and MSDOS.SYS, depending on whose version of DOS you're using) with backup copies from a different version of DOS.

/B:<date> restores only files that were created or changed on or before <date>. Enter <date> as you would for the Date command.

/A:<date> restores only files that were created or changed on or after <date>.

/M restores only files that have been changed since they were last backed up.

/N restores only files that don't exist on the target.

/E:<time> restores only files that were created or changed at or earlier than <time>. Enter <time> as you would for the Time command.

/L:<time> restores only files that were created or changed at or later than <time>.

Restore Examples

To restore the file named REPORT.DOC from the disk in drive A to its original location in the directory named \MKT\WP on the disk in drive C:

```
C>restore a: c:\mkt\wp\report.doc
```

To restore all files (the root directory and all subdirectories) from the disk in drive A to the same subdirectories on the disk in the current drive:

```
C>restore a: c:\ /s
```

To restore all files with the extension WKS from the disk in drive A to the directory named \SPREAD on the disk in the current drive, prompting for confirmation if the file has changed since it was backed up or if the file is marked read-only:

```
C>restore a: \mkt\wp\*.wks /p
```

Backing Up and Restoring Files with the Xcopy Command

As described in Part 5, the Xcopy command works like the Copy command, but does its job much faster and gives you much more selectivity in choosing the files to be copied. Although the Xcopy command wasn't designed specifically for backing up files, this selectivity lets you use the Xcopy command instead of the Backup and Restore commands to back up your hard disk. One advantage to using the Xcopy command is that it stores files in the normal fashion on the backup disk; files backed up with the Backup command can only be copied back to the hard disk with the Restore command.

The Xcopy command and its parameters are described in Part 5.

Xcopy Examples

The following examples duplicate the functions of the earlier Backup and Restore examples.

To back up all files whose extension is WKS from the current directory on the disk in the current drive to the disk in drive A:

```
C>xcopy *.wks a:
```

To back up all files whose extension is DOC from the directory named \WORD\MKT on the disk in the current drive to the disk in drive A:

```
C>xcopy \word\mkt\*.doc a:
```

To back up all files that have been modified since they were last backed up from the entire disk in the current drive (the root directory and all its subdirectories) to the disk in drive A, turning off the archive attributes of the files on the source drive:

```
C>xcopy \ a: /s /m
```

To back up all files whose extension is DOC from the current directory and all its subdirectories on the disk in the current drive to the disk in drive A, leaving the archive attribute of the backed-up files on the source disk unchanged:

```
C>xcopy *.doc a: /s /a
```

To back up all files whose extension is MSP that were changed on or after October 16, 1988, from the directory named \WIN on the disk in the current drive to the disk in drive A:

```
C>xcopy \win\*.msp a: /d:10-16-88
```

To back up all files from the current directory and all its subdirectories on the disk in the current drive, if the files were changed on or after October 16, 1988, and have not been archived since then, to the disk in drive A, turning off the archive attribute of the backed-up files on the source disk:

```
C>xcopy c: a: /m /s /d:10-16-88
```

To restore the file named REPORT.DOC from the disk in drive A to the directory named \MKT\WP on the disk in drive C:

```
C>xcopy a:report.doc c:\mkt\wp
```

or

```
C>copy a:report.doc \mkt\wp
```

To restore all files (the root directory and all subdirectories) from the disk in drive A to the disk in the current drive (drive D):

```
C>xcopy a:\ d:\ /s
```

To restore all files with the extension WKS from the disk in drive A to the directory named \SPREAD on the disk in the current drive, prompting for confirmation before each file is copied:

```
C>xcopy a:*.wks \spread /p
```

Backing Up and Restoring Files with Non-DOS Programs

Backup programs are available that copy files much more quickly than do the Backup and Restore commands or the Xcopy command. Some of these programs also compress the files as they back them up, to make the most efficient use of storage space, and expand the files when you restore them to the hard disk.

Just as with the Backup and Restore commands, these programs use special techniques to copy and store files. Thus, you usually cannot use the backup files they create as if they were standard DOS files; you must use the backup program to restore the files to the hard disk.

Some of the available programs, such as Fastback, let you choose from several options, all related to backing up a hard disk; others, such as PC Tools, package hard-disk backup with several other utility functions. A hard-disk backup program can be worthwhile if you must back up many files, especially if you back them up frequently.

Using a Tape Drive Instead of Diskettes

If you back up many files, and do so frequently, you may find yourself spending a lot of time backing up just because of the number of backup diskettes you have to juggle. A solution to this problem is to use a backup tape drive; the most common forms hold up to 60 MB, which should be sufficient for all but the largest hard disks and most stringent backup requirements.

Most backup tape drives are available as either an internal unit—which fits in the same space occupied by a disk drive—or an external unit, which sits beside the computer. The external units generally cost a bit more, because they require a separate case and power supply; the choice depends on whether your system has an empty drive bay and on how much space is available on your desktop.

Other storage devices can be used for backing up your hard disk, some of them more quickly than tape drives. Removable-cartridge hard disk drives, for example, offer the convenience of working just like any other hard disk; some models have two drives, so you can use one drive as your hard disk and the other as a backup unit. Less common cartridge tape units come with capacities of 120 MB or more, and offer greater speed as well as greater capacity.

But most of these systems tend to be more expensive than the more common tape drives, and many of them use their own methods of storing data, which means that you can exchange data only with someone who has an identical unit from the same manufacturer. In many cases, it would be cheaper to add a second hard disk drive to your computer, and use it to back up files from your primary hard disk.

CONTROLLING THE ARCHIVE ATTRIBUTE OF A FILE

In Part 5, under the heading "Preventing Accidental Changes and Deletions," you saw how to use the Attribute command to control the read-only attribute of a file or a group of files. If you're using 3.2 or a later version of DOS, you can also use the Attribute command to control the *archive attribute* of a file.

The archive attribute, like the read-only attribute, is part of the directory entry of a file. It isn't displayed by the Directory command, but it can be examined or changed by DOS or another program. This attribute is turned off by the Backup and Xcopy commands, and by some of the non-DOS programs that back up files. The attribute is turned on by Edlin, Microsoft Word, and most other programs that change a file.

The archive attribute, therefore, tells DOS—or any other program that checks it—whether a file has been changed since the last time it was backed up. The archive attribute is used principally by the Backup command, the Xcopy command, and backup programs, to determine which files should be backed up. You can control which files are backed up by turning the archive attribute on or off, but be careful not to prevent DOS from backing up files that should be backed up; you could defeat the purpose of backing up files in the first place.

Because of the way it is stored in the directory entry, you may sometimes see the archive attribute called the *archive bit*; rest assured the terms refer to the same thing.

The Attribute command, which lets you control the read-only and archive attributes, can have six parameters:

```
attrib +R -R +A -A <filename> /S
```

+R turns on the read-only attribute and -R turns it off.

+A turns on the archive attribute and -A turns it off. You can use these parameters with 3.2 and later versions of DOS.

<filename> is the name of the file whose attributes are to be changed or displayed. You can use wildcard characters to specify a group of files with similar file names or extensions.

/S tells DOS to apply the Attribute command to each subdirectory contained in <filename>. If you specify <filename> as *.* (all files on the disk beginning at the root directory) and include /S, the

Attribute command is applied to every file on the disk. You can use the /S parameter beginning with version 3.3 of DOS.

Attribute Examples

To turn on the archive attribute of the file named REPORT.DOC in the current directory on the disk in the current drive:

```
C>attrib +a report.doc
```

To turn off the archive attribute of all the files in the directory named \SPREAD on the disk in the current drive and do the same to all the files in its subdirectories:

```
C>attrib -a \spread\*.* /s
```

PART 7

Maintaining Your Hard Disk

A computer is made up of electrical and mechanical components. The mechanical portions, such as the keyboard, printer, and disk drives, are most prone to failure; the electrical portions simply don't have moving parts to wear out. (This isn't to say you can't have problems with the electrical portions, such as the memory or display adapter—just that any problems you experience are much more likely to arise from the mechanical elements.)

The hard disk drive has plenty of moving parts. The platters spin constantly; although the read/write heads don't contact the surfaces of the platters (at least under normal circumstances), they are frequently moved back and forth to the spots on the platters where information is to be read or recorded. Considering the amount of movement in a hard disk drive, today's systems are remarkably reliable; it's not unusual for a drive to hum away merrily for several years without a problem.

The high capacity and speed of the hard disk drive are possible because it is sealed in an airtight enclosure, so cleanliness isn't as important to the well-being of your hard disk as is the case with the keyboard or a diskette drive. But you can still help prolong the life of your hard disk drive and reduce the chance of problems. This section describes some steps you can take, most of which have two goals: reducing the amount of head movement, and minimizing the effect of physical shock.

But although these measures can reduce the likelihood of hard disk failure, don't be any less diligent about backing up your files. It's the unpredictability of failure that makes backup so important, regardless of how well you treat your system.

LEAVE THE SYSTEM ON

A computer, like a light bulb or a VCR, experiences a bit of extra stress each time you turn it on. You can prolong the life of your computer by turning it on and off as infrequently as possible. Computers don't require much electricity; leaving the system on doesn't cost much and will probably save you money over the life of the system by reducing maintenance costs.

Once you turn your system on, don't turn it off until you're through with it for the day. Don't, however, leave something displayed on the screen for hours at a time; turn down the brightness control or use a program that blanks the screen.

There's one exception to this practice. When you start using a brand-new computer, leave it on day and night for the first week or so. If something is going to fail, chances are it will fail early in its life. You want it to fail as quickly as possible so it can be repaired while the machine is still under warranty (and, in the case of your hard disk, before you have filled it with valuable files).

KEEP IT CLEAN

Cleanliness is the easiest preventive maintenance you can perform for your computer. You don't have to be a fanatic about it: Personal computers are fairly hardy, so the normal home or office environment is usually just fine. But the mechanical portions of the system will wear less if you keep them clean, and keeping the dust down lets the system run cooler.

Heat, in fact, is a natural enemy of the machine. Keep the temperature of the room comfortable for you, and don't lay anything on the display or system unit that blocks ventilating holes. Keep the dust down; you don't want a layer of dust to build up inside the machine, because it acts as an insulator and increases the operating temperature.

It isn't necessary to try for an antiseptic environment, but if there's a noticeable amount of dust where you use the computer, you can reduce the chance of a problem by putting a dustcover over the keyboard, display, and system unit when you're not using them. One of those expensive, custom-fitted covers isn't necessary; a piece of plastic or tightly woven nylon will do nicely.

WHAT ABOUT SURGES, SAGS, AND SPIKES?

The electric power from your wall plug isn't perfect. Sometimes the voltage rises a bit: a surge. Sometimes the voltage falls a bit: a sag. Occasionally there might be a momentary rise and fall of voltage as brief as a few thousandths, or even millionths, of a second: a spike.

Most of these anomalies go unnoticed, but a severe irregularity—a long surge or sag, or a particularly high spike—can cause your computer to reset or your hard disk to behave erratically. If this happens while the computer is reading from or writing to a disk, data on the disk—or even the disk itself—can be damaged.

You can buy a device called a surge suppressor to smooth out the variations in the power, but seek some advice before buying one; some of the cheaper ones don't offer much more than a false sense of security. And you may not need one at all—the power supplies in most IBM and IBM-compatible computers are remarkably tolerant of power fluctuations. If you have used your computer for several months and haven't noticed any erratic behavior, chances are that you don't need a surge suppressor. But if there are large industrial users of electricity in your neighborhood, or a power-hungry device, such as an air conditioner, is on the same circuit as your computer, or electrical storms are common in your part of the country, it might be a good idea to get a surge suppressor. Just be sure to get one that does the job.

A surge suppressor won't help, however, if the power goes off. For protection from power outages, you need something that continues to provide electricity itself. Such a device is called an uninterruptible power supply, or UPS. It switches to a battery-operated supply that provides 110 volts when the utility company power fails, and will run your computer for 10 to 20 minutes (depending on the size of its battery). A UPS isn't meant to be an alternate source of power; it simply keeps your computer running long enough for you to save files and shut the system down in an orderly fashion. Uninterruptible power supplies are rated in watts; 400 or 500 watts should be sufficient for a system with a hard disk, display, and printer.

MAKING LIFE EASIER FOR YOUR HARD DISK

A hard disk drive, like any other piece of machinery with moving parts, eventually wears out. Each time the drive reads or writes a file, it must move the read/write head to the proper position above the surface of the platter. Reducing the amount of such head movement can prolong the life of your hard disk. You can take two steps to cut down head movement: Take advantage of programs, such as RAM disk or disk cache (or both), that use the computer's memory as a temporary replacement for disk storage, and try to keep your files stored in contiguous sectors. These measures usually have the happy side effect of making file operations noticeably faster.

Substituting Memory for Disk Operations

Disk drives are mechanical, memory is electronic. Memory operations are faster, require less power, and don't cause wear and tear on moving parts. If you have enough available memory, dedicating a portion of it to a RAM disk (described under the heading "Using a RAM Disk" in Part 3) lets you transfer some disk operations to memory; just remember to copy all changed files from memory back to the disk drive before you shut down the system. (If you don't, you'll lose whatever changes you made to the files.)

In a somewhat similar fashion, a disk-cache program (described under the heading "Making Your Hard Disk Faster" in Part 3) substitutes memory operations for disk operations, but doesn't require you to explicitly save any files that have changed.

Some disk-cache programs, such as Lightning, write changed sectors to the disk as soon as you make a change to a file; while this eliminates some of the speed advantage of the cache, it protects you from losing work if the power should fail or the system go down while you're working. Other disk-cache programs don't write changed sectors to the disk until they need the memory where the changed sectors are stored or until you finish working with the file. Although this technique is faster, it exposes you to the possibility of lost work—or even lost files—if a failure occurs. If you're using a disk-cache program that doesn't update the disk whenever you make a change, be sure to save the file often to minimize the likelihood of problems.

If you don't have enough memory for either a RAM disk or a disk-cache program, consider adding more memory or making more memory available (for example, by eliminating some memory-resident programs that reduce the amount of available memory). You'll find that your system operates more quickly when it works with disk files—which is most of the time—and you'll be cutting down your disk drive's workload.

Dealing with File Fragmentation

If possible, DOS stores files in adjacent, or contiguous, sectors. As files are deleted and new files are stored, however, they can become fragmented—stored in nonadjacent or, as DOS refers to them, noncontiguous sectors. DOS can still use a file that is fragmented, but the disk drive must do more work: If a file is fragmented into three different groups of nonadjacent sectors, for example, the drive must move the head to each group of sectors to read the entire file.

As more and more files become fragmented, disk operations can be visibly slowed and the disk drive must move the head more than if the file weren't fragmented. You can restore files to contiguous sectors by backing up the entire hard disk, erasing all the files, and then restoring the files; it sounds time-consuming, and it is.

But you don't have to go through all this; several programs are available that let you pack all the files on a hard disk into contiguous sectors in a single operation. You make one selection from a menu and go do something else for a while—usually no more than 10 to 20 minutes—and let the program do the tedious work. One of the first such programs available is part of a package called the Mace Utilities; others include the Norton Utilities and Disk Optimizer.

The amount of disk fragmentation depends on what types of programs you use, how large your files are, and how often you use your computer. You can check disk fragmentation with the Check Disk program; if it shows a large number of files stored in noncontiguous sectors, pack the files. Doing this periodically reduces head movement and speeds program operation.

WHEN YOU MOVE YOUR COMPUTER

A hard disk contains delicate mechanisms, but is housed in an enclosure that protects it against mild bumps and shocks. You needn't baby the system, but treat it with the same care you would give a stereo or VCR. Don't be afraid to slide it across a desk or carry it from one desk to another, but be careful not to drop it or bang something else into it.

Pay particular attention when you move the system, especially if it will be carried in a truck or car; park the heads (more on that in a moment) and pack it in its original shipping container, including the foam or styrofoam cushions usually placed at the corners of the carton. (Also take these precautions if the hard disk drive must be removed from the system unit.)

Parking the heads means moving them to a position over an area of the platter where no data is stored. This way, if the drive should receive a shock that causes the head to bang against the surface of the platter, no recorded data will be damaged. Some drives automatically park the head each time you turn the system off, but others require that you park the head by running a program, usually called something like PARK.COM or MOVE.COM.

The documentation that came with your system should describe any precautions you should take when you move the system, including any specific instructions required to park the heads. Just like backing up your hard disk, taking a moment here is cheap insurance against a potentially damaging loss.

INSTALLING A NEW VERSION OF DOS ON YOUR HARD DISK

If DOS is installed on your hard disk and you want to install a newer version, you must copy two system files that DOS requires, as well as the DOS command and data files. This requires two commands:

1. The System command to copy the hidden DOS files.
2. The Copy command to copy the DOS command and data files.

The system files—IBMBIO.COM and IBMDOS.COM, or IO.SYS and MSDOS.SYS, depending on whose version of DOS you're using—are hidden files, so you don't see them in the output of the Directory command. You can copy them only with the System command. The System command has one parameter, the drive letter of the hard disk to which you want to copy the system files.

Example of Installing a New Version of DOS

Installing DOS on your hard disk requires only a few steps. The following procedure assumes that you have a directory named \DOS on the hard disk for the DOS files. If your DOS files are now in the root directory of the hard disk, create a directory named \DOS by typing *md c:\dos*, and follow the procedure as shown. After you have installed the new version, you'll have to delete the old DOS files from the root directory. If you keep your DOS files in some other directory, substitute the name of that directory for *dos* in steps 3 and 5.

To install a new version of DOS:

1. Put the DOS system diskette (labeled Startup or, in versions earlier than 3.3, simply DOS) in drive A, close the latch, and turn the system on (or, if the system is running, restart it by pressing Ctrl-Alt-Del).

2. When DOS displays the system prompt (A>), type the System command:

```
A>sys c:
```

DOS copies the two hidden files and responds *System transferred*.

3. Now copy the remaining files on the system disk with the Copy command:

```
A>copy *.* c:\dos
        22 File(s) copied
```

The number of files copied varies in different versions of DOS.

4. The file COMMAND.COM must be in the root directory of the hard disk, so copy it to the root directory and delete it from \DOS by typing the following two commands:

```
A>copy command.com c:\
        1 File(s) copied
A>erase c:\dos\command.com
```

5. If you're using 3.5-inch diskettes, you're done; go on to step 6. Otherwise, take the system diskette out of drive A, put it in a safe place, and put the second DOS diskette (labeled Operating or, in versions earlier than 3.3, Supplemental) in drive A. Copy these additional DOS files with another Copy command:

```
A>copy *.* c:\dos
        31 File(s) copied
```

Again, the number of files copied varies with different versions of DOS.

6. That's it. Now open the latch on drive A, so that DOS will start from the hard disk, and press Ctrl-Alt-Del. You should see the sign-on message of the new version you just installed. If you don't, go back to step 1 and repeat the procedure.

Index

A

ALLFILES.DAT 59–63
angle brackets *vii*
Append command 31, 36–37
archive attribute 75–76
ASCII file 49
Assign command, using caution with
    41, 42
Attribute command
    archive attribute 75–76
    read-only attribute 47–48
AUTOEXEC.BAT 14, 20, 35
    changing 39
    checking contents of 39
    required in root directory 37
    tailoring startup with 25–26

B

backing up your hard disk 65–76
    developing a procedure for 66
    DOS commands and 66–73, 75–76
    non-DOS programs and 73–74
    tape drives and 74
Backup command 66, 67–70
    BACKUP.00X 67
    caution about using 67, 70
    CONTROL.00X 67
    examples 69–70
    Join command and 41
    Substitute command and 42
BACKUP.00X 67
BAK 46
BAS 46
BAT 46
batch files 57–63
    FINDFILE.BAT 59–63
    MOVE.BAT 57–59
Bernoulli Box 1
binary file 50
buffer 16
Buffers configuration command 16–17

C

cache 23–24, 79–80
Change Directory command (cd) 31,
    32–33
clock/calendar 25
COM 46
COMMAND.COM 37–38, 40
command path 31, 35–36
    \DOS directory and 40
commands, DOS
    Append 31, 36–37
    Assign 41, 42
    Attribute 47–48, 75–76
    Backup 67–70
    Change Directory 31, 32–33
    configuration 16–23
        Buffers 16–17
        Device (with RAM disk) 20–23
        Files 15, 17–18
        Lastdrive 18–19
    Copy 48–51, 66
    Date 25
    Diskcomp 27
    Diskcopy 27, 41, 42
    Fastopen 24–25
    Fdisk 7–12
    Format 7, 12–13
    Join 41–42
    Label 27
    Lastdrive 15, 18–19
    Make Directory 30
    Path 31, 35–36
    Prompt 31, 33–35
    Remove Directory 31
    Replace 54–55
    Restore 41, 42, 67, 70–72
    Substitute 42–44
    Time 25
    Tree 55–57
    Volume 27
    Xcopy 48, 52–53, 72–73
CONFIG.SYS 15–22, 37
    changing 38–39

configuration commands. *See* commands, DOS
CONTROL.00X 67
conventions *vii*
Copy command 48–51, 66
CPI 47

D

Date command 25
directories
  changing 31, 32–33
  changing the way DOS treats 41–44
  creating 29–30
  current 31–35
    displaying 32
    in system prompt 33–35
  definition of 27
  DOS, creating 37–40
  moving to with .. entry 33
  path name 28
  removing 29, 31
  root 27
    AUTOEXEC.BAT 14, 20, 25–26, 35, 37, 39
    COMMAND.COM 37–38, 39–40
  setting up 28–29
  subdirectory 27, 29
disk
  buffer 16
  cache 23–24, 79–80
  cylinder 4
  partition 8
  platter 2
  sector 3–4, 80–81
  track 3–4
disk cache 23–24
Diskcomp command 27
Diskcopy command 27, 41
DOS. *See also* commands, DOS
  backing up files with 66–73
  configuring for hard disk 15–26
  directory 37–40
    adding to command path 39
    creating 37–38
    testing 39–40

DOS *(continued)*
  installing a new version on hard disk 82–83
  restarting 14, 40
DOS files, copying to hard disk 13–14
drive letter 18

E

Edlin 46
electric power, variations in 78–79
errorlevel
  values set by Backup command 68
  values set by Restore command 70
examples
  Attribute command 48, 76
  Backup command 69–70
  Change Directory command 32
  combining files 50–51
  Copy command 50–51
  Fdisk 9–12
  Format command 12–13
  installing a new version of DOS 82–83
  Join command 42
  Lastdrive command 19
  Make Directory command 30
  Path command 35–36
  Prompt command 34–35
  Remove Directory command 31
  Replace command 55
  Restore command 71–72
  Substitute command 43–44
  Tree command 56–57
  using a RAM Disk 22–23
  Xcopy command 53, 72–73
EXE 47
extended partition 8
extension 45–47
external hard drive 1

F

Fastopen command 24–25
Fdisk command 9–12
files
  access, speeding 24–25
  ALLFILES.DAT 59–63
  ASCII 49

files *(continued)*
  attributes
    archive 75–76
    read-only 47–48
  backing up
    with Backup 67–70
    with non-DOS facilities 73–74
    with Xcopy 72–73
  BACKUP.00X 67
  batch 57–63
    FINDFILE.BAT 57, 59–63
    MOVE.BAT 57–59
  binary 50
  COMMAND.COM 37–38, 40
  compression program 23
  CONTROL.00X 67
  copying 48–55
    with Copy 48–51
    with Replace 54–55
    with Xcopy 52–53
  copying DOS to hard disk 13–14
  extension 45–47
  FINDFILE.BAT 57, 59–63
  fragmented 80–81
  handle 17
  listing with Tree command 55–57
  moving with MOVE.BAT 57–59
  name 45–47
  preventing accidental change or
      deletion 47–48
  source 49–50, 52, 54, 59, 68
  target 49–50, 52, 54
Files configuration command 15, 17–18
FINDFILE.BAT 57, 59–63
Format command 7, 12–13
fragmented files 80–81

H

handle 17
hard disk
  backing up 65–76
    developing a procedure for 66
    DOS commands and 66–73, 75–76
    non-DOS programs and 73–74
    tape drives and 74
  copying DOS files to 13–14
  diagram of 2

hard disk *(continued)*
  formatting 7, 12–13
  identifying to DOS 8
  installing 4–5
  installing new version of DOS on
      82–83
  partition 8
  platter 2
  preparing 7–13
  storage capacity 2–3
  testing 14
  types of 1
heads, parking 81–82

I

index, in-memory 23–24
INI 47

J

Join command 41–42
  caution about using 41, 67, 68, 70
  examples 42

K

keeping track of where you are 31–37
  with Append command 36–37
  with Change Directory command
      32–33
  with Path command 35–36
  with Prompt command 33–35

L

Label command 27
Lastdrive configuration command 15,
    18–19

M

maintaining your hard disk 77–83
  changes in power level 78–79
  fragmented files on 80–81
  installing new version of DOS on
      82–83
  keeping system clean 78

maintaining your hard disk *(continued)*
  leaving system on 77–78
  moving 81–82
  using memory for disk operations 80
Make Directory command (md) 30
md command. *See* Make Directory
      command
MOVE.BAT 57–59

N

name
  file 45–47
  path 28

P

partition 8
Path command 31, 35–36.
path name 28
PIF 47
platter 2
power supply
  sags, spikes, and surges in 78–79
  surge suppressor 79
  uninterruptible (UPS) 79
primary DOS partition 8
Prompt command 31, 33–35
  showing current directory with 34–35

R

RAM disk 15, 19–23, 79–80
  defining 20–23
  RAMDRIVE.SYS 15, 20–22
  using 20
  VDISK.SYS 15, 20–22
RAMDRIVE.SYS 15, 20–22
rd command. *See* Remove Directory
      command
read-only attribute 47–48
Remove Directory command (rd) 31
Replace command 48, 54–55

Restore command 67, 70–72
  caution about using 41, 67, 68, 70
root directory 27

S

sag, power 78–79
sectors 3–4
  noncontiguous 80–81
side 3–4
source files 49–50, 52, 54, 59, 68
special extensions 46–47
spike, power 78–79
subdirectories 27, 29–30
Substitute command 42–44
  caution about using 41, 67, 68, 70
surge, power 78–79
surge suppressor 79
SYS 47
system prompt *vii*, 33–35

T

tape drive 74
target files 49–50, 52, 54
Time command 25
track 3–4
Tree command 55–57
  examples 56–57

U

uninterruptible power supply (UPS) 79

V

VDISK.SYS 15, 20–22, 40
virtual disk. *See* RAM disk
Volume command 27

X

Xcopy command 48, 52–53, 72–73

The manuscript for this book was prepared and submitted to Microsoft Press in electronic form. Text files were processed and formatted using Microsoft Word.

Cover design by Ted Mader & Associates
Interior text design by Greg Hickman
Principal typography by Carol Luke

Text composition by Microsoft Press in Times Roman with display in Times Roman Bold, using the Magna composition system and the Linotronic 300 laser imagesetter.